'899

The Harmony of Emptiness and Dependent-Arising

A Commentary to Tsong Khapa's

The Essence of Eloquent Speech, Praise to the Buddha for Teaching Profound Dependent-Arising

Published in commemoration of the 2550th Mahaparinirvana anniversary of Buddha Shakyamuni

Ven. Lobsang Gyatso

LIBRARY OF TIBETAN WORKS AND ARCHIVES

First Print: 1992
Revised Edition: 2005
Reprint: 2006, 2014

ISBN 81-86470-41-7

Published by the Library of Tibetan Works and Archives, Dharamsala and printed at Indraprastha Press (CBT), 4 Bahadur Shah Zafar Marg, New Delhi-110002

Contents

Contents

Acknowledgement

The author wishes to thank all of the people who assisted in the preparation of this work who by offering their time and energy in numerous ways serve as a fine illustration of how series of inter-related events can give rise to a successful result. Tushita Retreat Centre, Dharamsala, provided the setting and was responsible for the request that the teachings be given. Effie Hanchett and Sam Doharty undertook the task of recording the teachings which were translated by Sherab Gyatso. Effie took upon herself the work of transcribing and then Tenzin Losel assiduously edited the bulk of the material, assisted in later stages by L. Chophel Gangchenpa. Effie, Ngawang Palden, Gareth Sparham and Tenzin Tsepag shared the word-processing work.

Publisher's Note

This work by Ven. Lobsang Gyatso titled "*The Harmony of Emptiness and Dependent-Arising*" is a commentary to Tsong Khapa's "*The Essence of Eloquent Speech, Praise to the Buddha for Teaching Profound Dependent-Arising.*" The subject matter of the work concerns two central themes of Buddhist philosophy—emptiness and dependent-arising.

All schools of Buddhism expound theories of emptiness and dependent-arising, but their interpretations vary greatly and are even contradictory. Here the author very skillfully explains the complementary nature of the different schools and how they gradually lead to the highest school of thought—Prasangika Madhyamika. All explanations are given through logical analysis combined with simple yet wonderful examples.

This work is a welcome contribution in that it is by a meditation master who is a man of great learning and who has many years of practical teaching experience. We hope that the readers will gain profound analytical insight into the view of dependent-arising and thus be able to to proceed their journey on the Mahayana path to the state of great enlightenment.

We would like to thank to Ven. Lobsang Gyatso for this valuable contribution not only in the study of emptiness and dependent-arising but on Buddhism as a whole. Our thanks also goes to Losang Chophel Ganchenpa for proof-reading the material and for his suggestions.

Gyatsho Tshering
Director, LTWA

March 1992

The Root Text*

The Essence of Eloquent Speech, Praise to the Buddha for Teaching Profound Dependent-Arising.

---

*Root Text translator is not known.

Root Text

1.   I bow down to him whose insight and speech
Make him unexcelled as sage and teacher;
The victor, who realised (ultimate truth),
Then taught us dependently-related arising.

2.   Ignorance is the very root
Of all troubles in this transitory world.
These are averted by understanding
The dependent-arising which you have taught.

3.   How then could the intelligent
Not understand that the path
Of dependently-related arising
Is the essence of your teaching?

4.   This being so, O Saviour, who could find
Anything more wonderful
To praise you for
Than your teaching of dependent-arising?

5.   Whatever depends on conditions
Is empty of inherent existence,
What excellent instruction could there be,
More amazing than these words?

6.   Through wrongly holding (dependent-arising),
The childish strengthen bondage to extreme views.
But, for the wise, the same thing is the means
To cut free from the net of elaborations.

7.   Since this teaching is not found elsewhere,
      You alone are the 'Teacher.'
      For a Tirthika, this name would be a flattery,
      Like calling a fox a lion.

8.   O wondrous teacher! O wondrous refuge!
      Supreme speaker! Great protector!
      I pay homage to the great teacher
      Who so clearly explained dependent-arising.

9.   O benefactor! To heal all beings
      You proclaimed (dependent-arising),
      The peerless reason for ascertaining
      Emptiness, the heart of the teaching.

10.   How could those who see the way
      Of profound dependent-arising
      As contradictory or unproven
      Ever understand your system?

11.   When one perceives 'empty'
      As the meaning of 'dependent-arising,'
      Empty of inherent existence does not contradict
      The function of agent and action.

12.   Whereas if one perceives the opposite,
      Since there can be neither action in voidness
      Nor emptiness in what has action,
      One would fall into a dreadful abyss.

13.   Therefore understanding dependent-arising,
      As you have taught, is well praised.
      (Things) are not totally non-existent,
      Nor are they inherently existent.

14.   The independent is like a sky-flower.
      Therefore, nothing is not dependent.
      Existence with self-nature precludes
      Establishment by causes and conditions.

15. Thus it is taught that because nothing exists
    Other than the dependently-arisen,
    There is no existing thing
    Which is not empty of inherent existence.

16. Since inherent existence can never come to an end
    If phenomena had any inherent nature,
    Nirvana would be impossible,
    And all fabrications could not be stopped.

17. Therefore, who could challenge him
    Who, in assemblies of the wise,
    Has clearly proclaimed with lion's roar
    "Things do not have inherent existence."

18. Since lack of inherent nature,
    And the ability to function do not contradict,
    Never mind that dependent-arising
    And emptiness co-exist.

19. 'By the reason of dependent-arising,
    There are no grounds for extreme views.'
    For this fine teaching, O Protector,
    Your speech is unexcelled.

20. 'All is empty of self-nature!'
    And, 'From this cause arises that effect!'
    These two knowledges assist each other
    And abide in harmony.

21. What is more wonderful than this?
    What is more marvellous than this?
    If you are praised for this principle,
    That is real praise; nothing else.

22. Those held in slavery by delusions,
    Hopelessly resent you (so free and clear).
    Small wonder that they find intolerable
    That sound of, 'Non-inherent existence.'

23.   But to accept dependent-arising,
        The precious treasure of your speech,
        Then resent the roar of emptiness;
        This do I find surprising.

24.   If through the very term of highest
        Dependent-arising, the door that leads
        To non-inherent existence, they grasp
        Inherent existence, by what means

25.   Can these people be led into
        The good path which pleases you,
        That incomparable entrance,
        Well travelled by supreme Aryas?

26.   Inherent existence, unmade and non-dependent;
        Dependently-related, made and dependent;
        How can these two states be combined
        On one base, without contradictions?

27.   Therefore, whatever arises dependently
        Though always free of inherent existence,
        Appears to exist from its own side;
        So you said this is like an illusion.

28.   Through this very fact we can well understand
        The assertion that, in the way you taught.
        Those who would challenge you
        By way of logic can find no fallacy.

29.   Why? Because your explanation
        Makes remote the chance that one
        Will exaggerate or deny
        Manifest or non-manifest things.

30.   Your speech is seen as peerless
        Because it presents the path of dependent-arising,
        And this give rise to certainty
        That (your) other teachings are valid too.

31. You saw reality, and taught it well.
     Those who train in your footsteps
     Will transcend all trouble,
     For they shall destroy the root of evil.

32. But those who turn away from your teaching,
     Though they wearily struggle, long and hard,
     Are like inviting more problems
     As the view of self is further strengthened.

33. Marvellous! When the wise comprehend
     The difference between these two (trainings),
     How can they fail to respect you
     From their innermost hearts?

34. Not to mention the entire wealth of your teachings,
     Just a rough understanding of
     One small part of them,
     Is to bring supreme bliss.

35. Alas! My own mind was ruled by confusion
     Even though I took refuge long ago
     To such heap of qualities
     I do not possess even a part of the quality.

36. Yet before the stream of life has sunk
     Into the mouth of the Lord of Death,
     I have developed a little belief in you.
     Even this I think is fortunate.

37. Of teachers, the teachers of dependent-arising.
     Of wisdom, the wisdom of dependent-arising;
     These two are like kings conquering the world,
     Only you and no one else know this well and perfectly.

38. All that you have taught
     Is related to dependent-arising;
     And that also for transcending suffering.
     You perform no deeds that wouldn't bring peace.

39.   Wonderful is your teaching!
      Since whoever listens
      Will attain peace, who could not
      Be devoted to preserving such teaching?

40.   As it overcomes all opponents,
      Is free from internal contradiction
      And fulfills both goals of beings.
      My delight ever grows for this Doctrine.

41.   For the sake of this Doctrine, you gave
      Again and again over countless aeons,
      Sometimes your body, sometimes your life,
      Your dear family, and treasures of wealth.

42.   By seeing your qualities
      As a fish is drawn by the hook;
      How sad my fate to have not heard from you
      This teaching that you got so attracted.

43.   The intensity of this sadness
      Does not let my mind go free,
      Just as a mother's mind never separates
      From the thought of her beloved, lost child.

44.   But when I reflect on your speech, thinking,
      'Blazing with splendour of holy marks and signs,
      Haloed by rays of light,
      O Teacher, with your beautiful Brahma voice,

45.   You spoke in this way,' then in my mind
      The image of Shakyamuni arises and
      Immediately my sorrows are healed,
      As moon beams sooth a fever.

46.   Even with this marvellous and good system,
      The unskilled become totally confused,
      Just like an individual
      Who does not know how to untangle a *balbaza* grass

47. Seeing this I made every effort
    To follow the learned scholars,
    And repeatedly sought
    The meaning of your intention.

48. I studied many treatises
    Of Buddhist and non-Buddhist schools,
    My mind was then tormented sorely,
    Time and again in the web of doubt.

49. Nagarjuna was prophesied to explain rightly
    The principle of your final vehicle,
    Free from the extremes of existence and non-existence.
    His treatises are like a night lily garden.

50. One Whose bright orb of immaculate wisdom is fully developed
    Moving freely across the sky of scripture,
    Dispelling the darkness of extremist hearts
    And outshining the constellations of wrong speech.

51. Through the kindness of lama, When I see
    The illumination (of Nagarjuna's texts) by garlands of white
        light,
    The elegant explanations of glorious Chandrakirti
    My mind found relief and rest.

52. Of all his deeds, Buddha's speech is supreme,
    And, for this very reason, true sages
    Should commemorate the Perfect One
    For this (teaching of dependent-arising).

53. Inspired by the Teacher, I renounced the world
    And studied well the Conqueror's teaching.
    I have been diligent in yoga practice - such is
    This Bhikshu's reverence for the Great Seer.

54. By the kindness of my guru I was fortunate to meet
    The liberating teaching of the peerless guide,
    Therefore I dedicate this virtue as a cause
    For all beings to be received by spiritual friends.

55.   Until samsara ends, may the beneficent one's teaching
      Be undisturbed by the winds of wrong views;
      May all beings in the world forever understand
      The essence of the teaching and have faith in the teacher.

56.   May they uphold Shakyamuni's excellent way,
      Which reveals the principle of dependent-arising.
      Through all their lives let them never waver,
      Even at the cost of their bodies, or their lives.

57.   Day and night may they always be thinking
      How to best propagate this glorious success
      Achieved by the Supreme Liberator, in lives
      Of assiduous effort beyond measure.

58.   When beings strive with pure intention (to preserve
           this Doctrine),
      May Brahma, Indra, the world's protectors
      And the guardians, such as Mahakala,
      Be constant aides, never letting them down.

Commentary

by Ven. Lobsang Gyatso

I

Victorious

1. I bow down to him whose insight and speech
   Make him unexcelled as sage and teacher,
   The Victor who realized and taught
   Dependently related arising.

Tsong Khapa, the author of *The Essence of Eloquent Speech, Praise to the Buddha for Teaching Profound Dependent-Arising* is renowned as one of the very greatest scholar-saints that Tibet has ever produced. He wrote this text on the morning that he abandoned all perplexities and wrong views and for the first time experienced direct insight into reality which is the essence of Buddha's wisdom. Tsong Khapa was born in 1357 in the Tsongkha district of Amdo province in north-east Tibet.[1] From a very early age his life was wholly devoted to the study and contemplation of the Buddha's words and he single-mindedly pursued the highest and most inspiring of goals, the complete enlightenment of a Buddha, in order to be able to help all other beings free themselves from suffering. After many years of receiving teachings, study, debate, contemplation and retreat, during which he himself became famous as a teacher, one night in 1398 he dreamed that he was present at a discussion of the intricacies of the ultimate view between the most illustrious Buddhist masters of the past. One, whose commentary Tsong Khapa had been reading the previous evening, Buddhapalita, approached and blessed him by touching him on the head with a text. Thereupon Tsong Khapa awoke and turned again to Buddhapalita's commentary. As dawn was breaking he finally generated the blissful sun-like wisdom which experiences all things as they are and has the power to dispel forever the darkness of ignorance.

Praise for Dependent-Arising is Tsong Khapa's spontaneous outpouring of devotion to Shakyamuni Buddha for the unparalleled teachings which inspired and guided him through long years of practice and whose deepest truth he finally verified by his own direct realization on that morning. It is an expression of the author's redoubled faith in the Buddha, by its eloquence inspiring faith in others, drawing them into the study and practice of these teachings and setting them on the path which leads to the highest enlightenment. Tsong Khapa writes with a sense of fulfillment and precise certainty. With this assurance, his mind is turned completely towards benefitting all other beings in the world. If we could have an echo of this motivation in our minds as we read his verses and this commentary on them that would be excellent. Otherwise the contents of this book might become no more than a possible contribution to our general knowledge of the world. Reading to improve our general knowledge is fine, but when approaching dharma teachings ideally something more is called for. After all, the Sanskrit word dharma refers to instructions that hold us back from suffering. The Buddha showed how the cause of all the suffering we experience lies within, tracing it back to the deluded states of mind. Turbulent emotions such as jealousy, hatred, attachment and ignorant fanaticism are responsible for all harmful actions and consequent suffering. dharma teachings are designed to nourish the mind, to bring about attitudes of equanimity and compassion so that we can remain happy whatever the external conditions. With the powerful sword of wisdom, we can sever the root of all other delusions which is ignorance. In doing so, we will achieve the state of complete liberation from suffering. Even the Buddha, whose knowledge is unlimited, was once a human being and began by relying on the encouragement and teachings of others in the way that is now open to us. So dharma teachings are not designed merely to be a pleasant diversion but to be a powerful medicine. If the teacher can teach and the student can listen, or read, in this spirit, putting far away all thoughts of fame, praise, material gain and mere worldly knowledge, great benefit can ensue.

Besides the work under consideration here, *The Essence of Eloquent Speech, Praise to the Buddha for Teaching Profound Dependent-Arising*, Tsong Khapa wrote another work, which has the words 'essence of eloquent speech' in the title. The full title of that great work is *The Essence of Eloquent Speech, Treatise Distinguishing the Interpretable and*

Definitive. For this reason the verses we shall be discussing are sometimes known as the short *Essence of Eloquent Speech*, although we shall
use the abbreviated title, *Praise for Dependent-Arising* in this book. The
longer *Essence* presents a thorough evaluation of the different interpretations of the meaning of Buddha's deepest teachings that have
been put forward by various Buddhist scholars and practitioners. *Praise
for Dependent Arising,* as we shall see, a distillation of many of these
points which affords an excellent introduction to the central philosophical issue of the Buddhist path to liberation, the equivalence of
dependent-arising and emptiness.

In the first verse, Tsong Khapa, from all Buddha's good qualities,
singles out his realization and teaching of dependently-related arising.
The first verse is the expression of homage and Tsong Khapa bows
low to the one whose insight makes him unsurpassed in wisdom.
While other teachers teach from belief, from faith or teach wisdom
that comes in the form of dogma, Buddha taught from a complete,
direct understanding of his subject, and his theme is not something
that will only be of temporary passing benefit to his listeners but is
the wisdom which will release them completely from their burden of
misunderstanding and misconception. Nor is there anyone besides
the Buddha who taught dependent-arising so explicitly and so thoroughly, thus Buddha is unequalled in what he realized and what he
taught. How he taught is also regarded as unequalled in that he had a
special ability to teach in accordance with his listeners' predispositions
and needs. Through the completeness of his knowledge he understood
the individual listeners' capacities and skilfully taught according to
their level of understanding. This is reflected in the way Buddha's
teachings came to be grouped in the Indian and Tibetan traditions.
As we shall see, the teaching of dependent-arising has several different
levels of interpretation, each particularly helpful for a certain type of
person, but each superceded by a more refined and subtle presentation,
until the Buddha's actual final view is arrived at.

The Buddha's teachings are not the kind of teachings that are
merely attractive and pleasant to listen to, but they are able to bear
reasoned analysis. This is perhaps the distinguishing feature of Buddha's teachings concerning the way to liberation. All religions present
a path to a lasting kind of happiness, however it is called, but Buddha's

path does not merely depend for its authenticity on revelation or on spiritual authority, nor is the resultant state of happiness bestowed by a ruling deity. Rather, freedom comes when we remove the defilements of ignorance from our own minds, first by verifying with our own wisdom the truth of dependent-arising and then by applying that wisdom in concentrated meditation. The Buddha has many marvellous qualities, and faith towards such a being will yield an abundance of good effects, but the best possible, most stable basis for such faith is not merely to believe out of awe and admiration that he teaches authentic path to eliminate suffering but to establish it with reasoning. In the texts on valid cognition, the great Buddhist logicians Dignaga and Dharmakirti do this by establishing the validity of the first teaching the Buddha gave after his enlightenment, the teaching on the four truths, which will be discussed below. The highest school of Buddhist philosophers, called the Middle Way Consequentialists, however, take Buddha's unique and unmistaken presentation of dependent-arising as their prime example of a valid teaching, for it is on the basis of the teaching of dependent-arising, conjoined with the view of emptiness that Buddha became the triumphant victor, as he is praised by Tsong Khapa in the first verse.

Buddha is a victor because he has finally, completely and irreversibly vanquished the two obscurations and the four evil forces (maras.) The two obscurations are the obscurations of delusion and the obscurations to knowledge. The first is the name given to the mental defilements or ignorance that prevent us from attaining personal liberation. The second is the name given to the defilements which obstruct our mind from attaining the unlimited direct understanding of a Buddha. 'Mara' means demon or evil spirit in Sanskrit but in a Buddhist context such hindering influences are regarded principally as aspects of our own imperfect condition rather than as externally existing foes. The first mara, for instance, is the mara of the aggregates. Our aggregates are the parts which make us up, basically our body and mind. Obviously there are many advantages to having the kind of body we have, but the term, mara of the aggregates, with reference to the body, covers all the shortcomings having such a body entails. Having such a body renders us vulnerable to a huge variety of sufferings, of hunger, thirst, heat, cold, illness, tiredness, aches, pains and injuries, despite our constant attempts to cherish and attend to its every whim. Since our aggregates cannot be depended on and can hinder our progress in so many ways their unsatisfactory aspect is given the name mara.

The second of the maras is the mara of delusion, by which all negative states of mind such as anger, hatred, desirous attachment and pride are indicated. They are identified as a mara because they precipitate all harmful actions, from abusive speech to a mass murder. Not only that, when we are under the influence of a delusion it is most uncomfortable, such as when one boils with anger, and, unlike the suffering caused by an external enemy which lasts for the maximum of one lifetime, the seeds of delusion, unless we do something about them, stay in our mind and accompany it from lifetime to lifetime. All forms of conflict can be traced back to this internal enemy, the conflicts between nations, between members of a family and right down to the fighting and arguing that goes on between small children.

The third mara—Devaputra, son of a god— is something of an external troublemaker. As mentioned above, Buddhism identifies most causes of trouble as internal and shows that the remedy lies ultimately not in tinkering with the outside world but lies within. This mara, which is said to prey on beings who have a particularly strong resolve to achieve something positive, is something of an exception, but since it is also said to be dependent for its existence on people's superstition, the situation is not entirely cut and dried.

The last mara is the mara of death. Death is often personified as a particular being, the lord of death. This is a projection. What is intended here is the fact that we have to die soon enough, without knowing when and without the power to postpone it for a second. This great interrupter of life's hopes and aspirations is the fourth hinderance over which Buddha is completely victorious.

II

The Root of all Troubles

2. Ignorance is the very root
Of all troubles in this transitory world.
These are averted by understanding
The dependent-arising which you have taught.

All creatures are engaged in seeking happiness and trying to avoid suffering. Of those beings who are born with sufficient intelligence to be aware of their own motivation and have sufficient leisure to analyse what goals to aim at in life, many spend all their time in the pursuit of temporary forms of fulfillment, doubtful that there is any such thing as a permanent state of happiness, where suffering is completely abandoned. If pressed, these people may well admit that they suppose suffering, for instance in the form of old age, sickness and death, is ultimately inevitable and when such questions as, "Why are we here?" and, "Why is there dissatisfaction?" are posed their answer would be that, in these regions of investigation, man's lot is perplexity in the face of a mystery.

Those who have determinedly sought to penetrate this mystery have offered many paths of prayer and philosophy to the world, too many to be summarised properly here. There are those who have understood some aspects of the theory of karma, that we reap what we sow, in some form of future life if not in this, and make it their main practice to purify the seeds or potentials of bad actions they have previously committed, by confession, prayer or by voluntarily undergoing the hardship of physical penance. Others, tracing the origin of our problems back beyond the negative actions we have previously committed to the unwholesome conceptions that initiated them, principally endeavour to still the mind, to abandon all conception and eliminate discrimination as harmful in itself, in favour of some form of mental quietism. Others cultivate the practice of virtue. They practise generosity, patience and moral discipline. They live the life of love. The practice of benefitting others is most certainly supremely important, but thinking that that, by itself, is the whole path to the highest happiness in this or a future existence is mistaken, and the same applies to the other two types of practice we have mentioned. They are mistaken according to Tsong Khapa because, without understanding the profound dependent-arising, one cannot gain the ultimate view, without familiarising oneself again and again with the ultimate view, one cannot destroy ignorance; without destroying ignorance, one cannot find release from the sufferings of this transitory world, nor can one attain the enormous beneficial potential of a fully enlightened being. Hence the utterly essential need to understand dependent-arising, set forth in many different ways by the Buddha and condensed and celebrated here by Tsong Khapa.

We will thus be extremely fortunate if we can find a teacher who can explain dependent-arising to us flawlessly, for even within Buddhist philosophy there are a variety of different treatments of this central issue. Our way to proceed will be by bringing together the teachings of a living master or masters, and our own analysis and study of the Buddhist texts. There are four Buddhist schools, called the Particularists, the Sutra-followers, the Proponents of Mind Only and the Proponents of the Middle Way. The last school has two divisions, the Autonomists and the Consequentialists.[2] The explanation of dependent-arising reaches its fullest power in the commentaries of the Consequentialists whose foremost exponent in the Land of Snow was Tsong Khapa. Briefly at this stage, the schools of Mind Only and below only understand dependent-arising in terms of effects dependent on their causes, taking no account of uncaused or permanent i.e. unchanging phenomena. The Middle Way Autonomists extend the meaning of dependent-arising by showing how all phenomena, caused and uncaused, exist within the nature of dependent-arising, in the sense that they depend on their parts. For instance, a pot is not self-powered; it depends for its existence on its causes. Also it depends on its parts because, without perceiving the parts of a pot, one cannot perceive a pot. The Consequentialists accept the above viewpoints but add various perspectives of their own, arguing that cause and effect are mutually dependent, as are self and other, and further reinterpret all other forms of dependent relationship in the light of their being dependently arisen in the sense of being mere imputations, upon a basis of designation, by a designating consciousness.

The above brief review of dependent-arising's various manifestations in the various schools of Buddhism maps out part of the route our investigation will take in later chapters. However, before we discuss how to cultivate the wisdom understanding dependent-arising, the antidote which will eliminate all our suffering, we first have to justify the diagnosis that ignorance is the primary cause of the disease, 'The root of all troubles in this transitory world.' First we will base our investigation on the teaching of the four truths and second on the teaching of twelve links of dependent-arising.

THE FOUR TRUTHS

If someone is ill, in order to treat the person and make him well, the doctor first has to take careful note of the symptoms of the disease and from them determine its root causes. Just administering medicine to relieve the symptoms will not do; the patient wants a remedy that will cure the disease completely and bring him to sound health. Having made his diagnosis, the doctor then prescribes a course of treatment appropriate to the disease which is designed to get rid of it. Finally the patient follows the doctor's instructions and is cured. This analogy serves well to introduce the four truths and their sequence. According to the analogy we are the patients and our condition is known as true suffering, which is the first of the truths. True suffering refers to all the trouble we face, all the forms of pain and dissatisfaction we encounter in this round of existence. However exalted our worldly status, we have to endure physical pain and mental anxiety. We do not escape the pangs of birth, aging, sickness and death. We never seem to be satisfied; we may have what we need, but we always crave for more. If we get what we desire, after enjoying it for a while we start to hanker after something else. If we do feel we are happy at a certain moment, we have to acknowledge the unsatisfactory feeling that, in the nature of things, we are bound to undergo suffering again, sooner or later.

The troubles of this world are easy to enumerate at length. Searching for their ultimate source, like the doctor trying to determine the root cause of the patient's illness, is more of a challenge. The causes of true sufferings are what are known as true origins, the second of the four truths. There are two divisions of true origins, karma, or action, and delusion. The first, karma, arises in dependence on the second, delusion. Delusions are various, attachment, hatred, pride, envy and so forth, the ultimate source of them all being, as Tsong Khapa says, ignorance. This, the second of the four truths is the one we are going to dwell on in this presentation of the four. In outline, the third truth is true cessation. It is synonymous with liberation, the final abandonment of suffering. In our medical analogy it is equivalent to the state of good health the sick person wishes to achieve. In other words it refers to the goal of religious practice or philosophy. The fourth truth is true paths. True paths refers to the realisations which are the antidote to the ignorance which is identified as true origins. They are thus like treatment prescribed by the doctor once he has properly identified his patient's illness. Those who have gone to liberation did so by generating these realisations in their minds.

Returning to the second truth, true origins, how ignorance is responsible for all the problems we encounter can be illustrated with the example of the effects of killing. The ignorance in question, the ignorance concerning dependent-arising, has two main aspects, ignorance of karma and ignorance of the ultimate nature of phenomena. The ignorance concerning the workings of karma will be described first.

There are those who actually enjoy killing, such as hunters or fishermen who regard killing as sport. There are butchers too, who enjoy killing and do it with enthusiasm, thinking of the profit they will obtain from selling the meat of their victims. To such a one the effect of killing is happiness; he deliberately engages in the action in the expectation of pleasure. It may well be that in the short term his expectations are fulfilled; the hunter enjoys his meal or his stuffed trophy and the butcher his profits. The long term effects of their actions are, however, far from being pleasurable, according to the principles of karma, the first of which states that actions are never wasted; they are certain to produce similar consequences, possibly in this life; usually in a future life.[3] Those who take life will experience suffering proportionate to the suffering they inflicted and the degree of enthusiasm with which they inflicted it. One who commits very harmful actions is liable to take rebirth in a lower state of existence, hellish or ghostly for instance, or if the action is less intensely negative, he may take an animal rebirth. Other consequences may also flow from his act of killing. Even if he is born in a higher realm, his life span may be very short and he may have the inclination or tendency to enjoy taking life again and again. On the other hand there is always the possibility of purifying negative karma through the appropriate Dharma practices, in which case none of the above consequences are absolutely certain to occur. Much too depends on the strength of motivation. In our example we painted a picture of a very strong negative motivation which would incline those beings to be born in a hellish existence, but one can kill accidentally and it is not altogether impossible to kill with a virtuous motivation, free of self-cherishing. In these circumstances, the negative action of killing would still be committed but the ripened effects of the action would no doubt be lighter. The way the ripened effects of different actions can blend together is another variable. Here we are referring to what are known as projecting karma and completing karma. The projecting karma from an act of killing might for instance project or throw us into a lower state of existence, such as being born as a dog. Then completing karma deriving from a previous positive action might ripen during that life as a dog such that we are sheltered by kind people who provide us with excellent food and other comforts. Similarly, good projecting karma can bring about a higher state of rebirth only for it to be complemented by miserable completing karma.

Basically, all the pleasure we experience comes about due to our having committed virtuous actions, actions which benefit others, and all the suffering we experience comes about due to our having accumulated non-virtuous or harmful actions. The butcher of our example does not understand the true nature of the situation and he grasps that the action of killing will bring him pleasure and profit. Neither knowing nor caring about the long-term effects of his actions, snatching at the temporary pleasures of this life and indulging in the negative passions of greed and self-cherishing, he is whirled again and again into the troubles of this transitory round of existence, a leaf blown by the wind of his karma or past actions.

It is crucial for us to contemplate this facet of dependent-arising very carefully and gain conviction concerning the principles of karma. One who does can then determine firmly to abandon the taking of life. The firmer the decision the better; there is a much stronger beneficial effect from not killing having actively determined not to do so than from merely happening not to kill. The former is an actual wholesome or virtuous action whose effect will be happiness, possibly leading to a future rebirth in one of the higher realms, as a human with a spark of intelligence, or amongst the gods who enjoy again and again the pleasures of refined sense gratification or the bliss of exalted states of meditative stabilization. But even those who are born in these worldly divine realms have not escaped suffering for good. They have not overcome the mara of death, for instance. In due course their happiness will come to an end. They will experience the trauma of death and rebirth again and migrate to another life, and yet another. A person who is still ensnared by false notions of the self, the root cause of suffering, and is ignorant of the power of the antidote, meditation on dependent-arising and selflessness, although he may have a correct understanding of karma which leads him to abandon killing, he has not entirely overcome the mara of delusion. His desires still remain focused on cyclic existence.

By contrast there is the person who, with the additional guidance of some understanding of the ultimate nature of the self, develops a pure and powerful wish to take control and free himself from the whole unsatisfactory round of death and rebirth powered by delusion and unskilful action. The clarity of the insight that Tsong Khapa attained on the morning that he composed this praise is such that the ignorance which throws us again and again into misery cannot abide simultaneously with it, no more than heat and cold can exist on the same spot. The ignorance is forced to give way just as the darkness in a room vanishes when we turn on the light. For somebody who has recognized the power of such wisdom and has thereby generated an authentic determination to emerge from cyclic existence, the effects of his action of decisively refraining from killing are in accordance with this strong wish and lead not to further involvement in the world but out of it, to liberation.

Abandoning killing in the hope gaining release from cyclic existence is still not the highest motivation we can aspire to. We can abandon killing and experience some form of pleasure within cyclic existence. Beyond that we can abandon killing as part of our efforts to gain our own individual liberation from it, but best of all is to abandon killing with the pure wish to be of the utmost benefit to as many sentient beings as possible. One dwells on the fact that sufferings descend on all creatures alike, not just on oneself, and contemplates that a Buddha is the one who has the highest wisdom and most skilful means to separate beings from their sufferings. Then one develops the spontaneous resolve to become a Buddha oneself for the benefit of all. This is called bodhicitta or the mind of enlightenment. When coupled with the precious bodhicitta in this way, the virtuous action of abandoning killing contributes to our own achievement of Buddhahood. Buddhahood is the highest enlightenment because it is for the sake not of oneself alone but for all sentient beings.

Depending on our motivation then, the long-term results of our virtuous actions such as avoiding harming others or generosity can either be worldly pleasure, the happiness of individual liberation or the fulfilment of complete enlightenment. Whether we can develop the more worthwhile second or third levels of motivation depends on whether our minds are obscured or not with regard to the ultimate nature of the self and phenomena. If it is, then the effects of all our actions, whether virtuous or non-virtuous, will ripen as further experiences within cyclic existence. In this sense our ignorance can be called the creator of the world. The Indian Middle Way master Aryadeva said in *The Four Hundred*,

> Ignorance pervades all delusions,
> Just as the physical sense faculty resides throughout the
> body.
> Thus when ignorance is destroyed,
> All other delusions will be destroyed too.

On the other hand, the wisdom which dispels such ignorance, the wisdom understanding ultimate nature, which is generated from our understanding of dependent-arising, is said to be the creator of the states of liberation and enlightenment. Some Buddhist schools in fact say that karma is the creator of the world. The highest school, the

Consequentialists say that it is the mind or ignorance. These explanations are not contradictory. To give an analogy, karma can be likened
to the soldiers who perform the acts of shooting and killing in a battle,
while ignorance can be likened to the president of a country who
orders his troops to war. We can point out fingers at the soldiers and
say they did the killing but equally we can say that the ultimate
responsibility for those acts lies with the president. In any case, when
tracing back to the ultimate cause of the world, Buddhist thought
goes back no further than our own minds. Buddhist thinkers have
found no place for a creator-being, an architect or prime mover who
of his own volition brings forth the universe. The source of our
problems lies within our own minds, and so does the remedy. This is
the import of the Buddha's teaching of the four truths.

Twelve Links of Dependent-Arising

A brief reference to another of the Buddha's teachings, the twelve
links of dependent-arising, should further open the way to understanding the benefits of realizing dependent-arising that Tsong Khapa
celebrates in this praise. We will recognize these benefits when we
understand more clearly about the nature of cyclic existence. Cyclic
existence refers to life in those worlds or realms, such as ours, in which
suffering occurs. Every state within it is transient and unstable. It is
characterized as a round wheel because we are born here again and
again. We are bound to the wheel of existence because our births here
are under compulsion and the cycle is very difficult to get rid of. The
twelve links of dependent-arising are often drawn or painted in the
form of a wheel, held fast in the embrace of Shinje, the Lord of Death.
The twelve links are (1) ignorance; (2) compounded karma;
(3) consciousness; (4) name and form; (5) six sources; (6) contact;
(7) feeling; (8) desirous attachment; (9) grasping; (10) existence;
(11) birth; (12) aging and death.

The first of the twelve links is ignorance, and the root ignorance
is ignorance concerning the ultimate nature of phenomena. Under
the influence of this ignorance, a person commits an action, whether
positive, negative or neutral, and this action forms the second link,
compounded karma. Until it ripens in a future lifetime or later in
this one, this action is, as it were, stored in the consciousness in the

form of a potential or seed. Consciousness is the third link, and it is like the earth in which a seed rests until the other conditions necessary for it to germinate come together. If a seed is to germinate, one condition it certainly needs is moisture. In the case of the karmic seed, the equivalent of moisture is desirous attachment, attachment to the forms and features of cyclic existence with which one has such an ingrained familiarity. In the sequence of twelve links, attachment is placed eighth, but it is to that one we must now jump in this condensed explanation of the twelve links in terms of two lifetimes. The attachment particularly referred to here is the attachment to some feature of cyclic existence that manifests in the mind of someone who is on the verge of death. The next link, the ninth, grasping, is when that attachment strengthens up. As a person's gross sense consciousness shut down at death, there arises a strong inclination for a particular type of rebirth, as a certain kind of animal, as a human, a god or whatever. Appearances are said to arise to the mind of the forms or birth places the mind is attracted towards and will be associated with. The tenth link is called existence and refers to that fully potentialized karma, or action, which throws a person into a new life. The action of the second link has now ripened up, now all the conditions, such as attachment have come together. The six links we have mentioned so far, the first, second, third, eighth, ninth and tenth are, in this presentation, a causal sequence and the link of existence is the last moment of that sequence. The relationship between the body and mind of the person in that particular life now ceases. The consciousness departs from one life and goes on to the next.

The next link in the twelve, the first of the effect sequence, is birth, although between the end of one life and the start of another there is an intermediate stage. In this in-between state one has a body but is such a subtle type of form that it is not obstructed by gross matter such as walls and so forth, and it is not visible to ordinary eyes, although it is said to bear some resemblance to the form of the type of being one will become in the next life. We can think of radio broadcast being transmitted from the radio station to the place where someone is listening to the radio. Something travels from the broadcasting station to the receiver. It is not sound. We could say it is the potential to produce sound. The force which causes the radio waves to travel from one place to another in our illustration is like the fully potentialized karma in terms of the twelve links. When the sound waves reach a receiver, various sounds come forth. Similarly the force of karma propels a consciousness together with its very subtle energy body to a new place of birth where it unites with a new body of gross form, the joining sperm and egg of the mother and father in the case of human and most animal births, and arises as a new creature. Strictly speaking, however, the link of birth begins with the adoption of the body of the intermediate state right after death.

Of all the actions we have done whose effects have not yet worked themselves out, only one, the one ripening just at death, is responsible for determining what broad kind of rebirth we will experience. Why should one particular action, and not another, ripen up at this crucial time? Some actions leave a trace on the mind that is too weak ever to ripen up. Some actions are more liable to ripen up because the impression they left on the mind was sharp and strong. There is also the factor of how familiar we are with a certain action. The more familiar we are with a particular action, the more likely it is that it will be the strongest at the moment of death and the one that steers us to our new world. Can the consciousness and body separate other than at the time of death? Yes, this can occasionally happen. There is a type of separation, if not a complete one, that can occur in sleep. There are also special techniques of meditation and concentration that enable an adept deliberately to separate the two, but for most people, when their mind and body come apart, it means they have reached the end of their life.

To continue with our enumeration of the twelve links, from birth, the eleventh link, we shift to the link of name and form, the fourth on the wheel of twelve and the second of the effect links. The link of name and form begins when the consciousness joins with its new form or body. After this comes the stage at which the sense powers (five physical and one mental) arise in the unborn creature. This is called the link of the six sources.[4] The six sources are the fifth link and contact is the sixth. With the stage of contact the sense consciousnesses, the eye consciousness, the ear consciousness and so forth, start to have involvement with their objects. The subtle consciousness which entered the womb has given rise to gross levels of consciousness once more and these have their avenues of communication, the sense powers. They make contact with their objects and then the seventh link, feeling, occurs. All the while the process of aging has been going on and death has been approaching. Aging and death constitute the twelfth and final link. Another circuit of the wheel of existence comes to an end when the twelfth link's second stage, death, is complete. When life cannot be prolonged any further, the gross consciousness dissolves back into the subtle, the mind leaves its old body and heads towards the next life.

In terms of this present life, in the life prior to this one, we created the first three links, ignorance, compounded karma and consciousness, and also links eight, nine and ten: desirous attachment, grasping and existence. These are the six causal links which brought about this life. The remaining six links: four, name and form; five, six sources; six, contact; seven, feeling; eleven, birth and twelve, aging and death are the six effect links which we are now passing through in this life. Only the final portion of the final link, death, has not been completed yet. Of course we are accumulating many different actions all the time. Any of these actions that are strong enough can give rise to a future birth, be it in a human realm, an animal realm, a hell realm or any other realm. We are continually creating causes for being reborn again. Even now, while we are experiencing the six effect links as we have just indicated, we are also going through the six causal links that will culminate in the next life. It is impossible to point a finger and say, 'This is the start of it all.' This beginningless round is what is referred to by the term cyclic existence or samsara. It is a process of continually creating karma and being reborn. All the four Buddhist schools we named earlier accept the description of the round of existence contained within the teaching on the twelve links of dependent-arising and the four truths. We should meditate upon it repeatedly in order to generate the mind determined to emerge from it. If we do, we will be drawn again and again to probe the ignorance that is 'the very root of all troubles in this transitory world,' and to wonder just what is the understanding of dependent-arising which shatters it asunder.

We have already noted that these verses are a spontaneous expression of Tsong Khapa's gratitude to the teacher Shakyamuni Buddha composed on the morning that he first gained a pure direct realization of the highest Buddhist view. All wrong views cast aside and inspired by the deepest faith, he prostrates and offers praises to Buddha, thus adding to the great wave of positive or meritorious energy that will carry him to the state of highest enlightenment. The poem will only achieve its complete purpose, however, if many of us too have our admiration awakened for a noble teacher and his penetrating teachings, and have a strength of conviction that will carry us through our studies, at least to the point where we become fully convinced of the validity of the endeavour and the worthiness of attaining the goals, individual liberation or full enlightenment.

3.   How then could the intelligent
      Not understand that the path
      Of dependently related arising
      Is the essence of your teaching?

4.   This being so, O Saviour
      Who could find anything
      More wonderful to praise you for
      Than your teaching of dependent-arising?

While we contemplate the disadvantages of all states of rebirth in the cyclic existence in order to turn away from its superficial allurements, we should exert effort in thinking about the advantages of the peaceful state of liberation in order to make the wish to go there our strongest urge. The mind which understands dependent-arising is itself the path of verse three. A path we generally understand as a way we walk along to get to a certain destination. In the present context it is apt to call the mind which realizes dependent-arising a path because, once we have cultivated it, familiarising again and again on it, dwelling on that mind in meditation, is the way we travel to liberation. Dependent-arising is thus the essence of the teaching because realization of it is the key to becoming free from cyclic existence and going to enlightenment, as those who have turned their minds away from cyclic existence and have gained an understanding of dependent-arising, 'the intelligent,' surely know. This is why Tsong Khapa praises Shakyamuni Buddha above all for this wonderful gift of teachings on this topic. While other philosophers and practitioners pursue the same goal of highest happiness, of the hosts of teachers and guides, only the Buddha reveals the technique of dependent-arising, unsurpassed in effectiveness, and of the Buddhist schools, only the Consequentialists are able to explain it in all its magnificent depth and clarity. To do justice to the profundity of Tsong Khapa's verses, it is to an illumination of these assertions that we must now proceed, beginning with the views of the other schools, Buddhist and non-Buddhist, that the Consequentialists either refute or surpass.

III

Cause and Effect

5-ab Whatever depends on causes and conditions
     Is empty of inherent existence.

Consider first how we ordinarily grasp things to exist. Do we not feel
that the self and the everyday objects around us are established from
their own side, that 'I' and the objects I use and possess are each
substantial, solid, 'concretely pointoutable' entities? We can experience
a sense of ourselves existing from our own side very vividly when we
are in a perilous situation such as when we go to too near the edge of
a steep cliff. At that time do we not appear to ourselves to exist by our
own power, solidly and independently, having a nature that exists
from within ourselves? But all our everyday perceptions are also tinged
with this type of grasping. When we glance at our watch, for example,
does it not appear to have its own independent, self-sufficient nature
over and above any relationship that may be said to exist between it
and other phenomena?

The Middle Way Consequentialists argue that all phenomena
arise in dependence on causes and conditions and are therefore not
established from their own side, do not exist by way of their own
entity and are not inherently existent. Understanding this thoroughly
is the way to remove the troubles of this transitory world. Apart from
the Consequentialists, however, most schools of thought, Buddhist
and non-Buddhist, western and eastern assume that phenomena do
exist inherently, in the way that they appear.

Christians accept that the world was created by God, while God's
existence on the other hand is not under the influence of causes and
conditions. If the creation of God is discussed at all the answer would
seem to be that he is eternal or self-created. Many Hindu traditions
adopt a similar point of view, crediting the creation of the world to a

deity, Ishvara, who himself is unaffected by causes and conditions and who abides beyond fluctuation and instability. So both Christian and Hindu philosophers point to cause and effect relationships when trying to explain how things came about and how they exist. Tracing the causes backwards they arrive at a primordial being who stand outside the realm of change, an ultimate source from which all other phenomena derive their truly or inherently existent natures. The Hindu schools who accept rebirth view the I or self in a similar fashion. According to their reasoning we observe ourselves working, reading, eating and so forth. Then, tracing all these actions back to their source, we arrive at the self. It is the I which causes all these actions to be performed. The source of our actions, they argue, has to be something substantial, truly existent, even unchanging. If the I is forever changing, they say, how can we speak of an I that goes from one life to another?

However, if we look into the implications of these assertions, for instance that there is such a thing as a creator deity who does not change, or that the I is permanent or unchanging, we will find that they create rather more problems than they solve. Are not the God before the creation of the universe and the God who has created the universe necessarily different? And is it not a case of the former changing into the latter, in the same way that a childless woman has to change in some way in order to become a mother? A God that is beyond change and a God that is the creator of the universe are therefore incompatible. The idea of an unchanging I is similarly problematic. Unfortunately there are many intelligent people these days who have come across one or two defective systems of thought and have identified many faults. This has discouraged them and led them to forsake the study and practice of religion and philosophy entirely.

A world view very familiar to Westerners who are coming into contact with Buddhist ideas these days is that formed under the influence of scientific discoveries and techniques of investigation, so a few comparative remarks about science and Buddhism may not be amiss for Westerns approaching the topic of dependent-arising. In their practical application Buddhism and science may be strikingly different, but in terms of view there are many explanations where the two systems are in accord, differing in emphasis rather than in fundamentals. Whereas science has been most successful in uncovering the workings of external phenomena such as matter, Buddhism's focus has always been on internal phenomena, namely on the mind. Obviously scientific investigation has revealed things that Buddhism has not touched upon and vice versa but it would be difficult to point to a subject where the two systems' assertions actually clash. This gives grounds for supposing that as research and investigation continue the two ways of thought could come closer together.

If we compare the theories of the origin of the universe and its contents presented in the scientific and Buddhist traditions a similar view of the process emerges. Various explanations of how this world, the other planets and the stars originated are put forward in different scientific theories, a common theme of which seems to be that though a beginning can be posited for the various heavenly bodies and so forth, the process of becoming in the universe in general is not something which scientists can state had a particular beginning. Whatever phenomena they trace back to, itself in turn must have had a cause. Down on the atomic level we find the same broad conclusion obtaining. Many minute particles temporarily conglomerate to form a material object which then in the fullness of time disintegrates. Individual gross forms arise and fall apart or are destroyed, but it is not possible to posit a beginning to the process. Any atomic substance or element has to have a cause. That cause must also have a cause and so on. Buddhist scholars have no quarrel with all this; rather they extend this understanding to the mind. Just as it seems simplest to say that matter has always been around in one manifestation or another so, we say, has mind, basically for the same reasons.

The scientific description of the conception and development of a child in the womb deals principally with the manifest physical aspects, from the meeting of the sperm and ovum onwards, whereas the Buddhists, while not faulting this explanation, bring three other elements to the fore, consciousness, subtle form and karma. A consciousness which has some time previously separated from its former body, and which contains the karmic seeds or potentials deposited on it by previous actions, together with its support, a very subtle kind of form, enters the womb at the time of conception and joins with the uniting sperm and ovum, its new body. As the child grows in the womb, science can furnish a very accurate picture of the different stages of its physical development. The Buddhist texts speak more about the inner experience of the child during this time. Again, these two versions of the first stage of life would seem to be quite compatible. The points of view are different but there is nothing in the Buddhist description which contradicts the scientific one and the Buddhist finds the scientific description complementary to his own.

Mind is in essence clear and cognizing. The only thing which can become the entity of the present moment of any individual's mind—and this includes the mind of an individual at the first moment of conception— is the previous moment of that mind. How can something which does not have the qualities of being clear and knowing and does not experience happiness and sorrow change into something which is clear and knowing and does experience happiness and sorrow? Matter cannot be produced in the entity of something clear and cognizing. Each individual's mind is a non-material phenomena which does not have any beginning; nor does it have any end. Everyone's stream of consciousness is constantly changing. Sometimes such a stream of consciousness takes a gross form, the ordinary sense consciousnesses being considered gross. Sometimes it takes a subtle form, for instance during the death process. Sometimes the delusions such as anger, hatred and pride flare up. Sometimes they are not manifest, existing only as potentials. The influence of ignorance is always present to some degree in an ordinary person's consciousness; affecting every cognition such a person has. Associated with every consciousness and acting as its basis is a very subtle kind of form or energy called subtle wind. Like the mind it accompanies, it cannot be said to have any beginning. Nor indeed can we who, as it were, possess our particular stream of consciousness be said, in a sense, to have any beginning. A person in this sense of the world goes from life to life, sometimes being born in the human realm, sometimes being born as animal or else as a god or some other creature. The gross physical forms are adopted and discarded while the consciousness migrates on and on from one existence to another. Upon death, anyone who has not mentally evolved to the point where he or she can step off this round will be thrust yet again into an existence where suffering occurs.

The main goal of dharma practice is to bring to an end the process of uncontrolled rebirth because what it amounts to is suffering. The means lies in our capacity for mental evolution. Hence the main subject for analysis and investigation in Buddhist philosophy is the mind. If we briefly mention one or two of the major classifications of mind in the Buddhist system there is first of all the division into two, valid and non-valid awarenesses, those that correctly apprehend a particular aspect of reality and induce certainty with respect to it and those that do not.[5] A careful study of these two types of mind is most worthwhile. For instance, an investigation of valid minds reveals two distinct kinds, direct valid perceivers and inferential valid cognizers. Some of the key objects of contemplation and meditation on the path to liberation such as emptiness and dependent-arising are quite subtle affairs so an ordinary being cannot observe them by direct perception, though that is his eventual aim. To understand them in the beginning he has to depend on an inferential cognition which is basically the type of infallible mind which relies on a reason. To give a simple example of an inferential cognition: suppose we are standing outside a house and we see smoke rising from the chimney. In dependence on cognizing smoke we can infer that there is fire or combustion inside the house. We cannot see the fire directly but we can have accurate knowledge of it by relying on a correct sign, smoke. The first type of wisdom that we cultivate to guide us on the path to liberation will be of this type which depends on reasons, so a particularly carefully study of this kind of mind is found in the Buddhist texts. The exactness, thoroughness and helpfulness of the Buddhist treatises on psychology could easily be illustrated with many examples but perhaps enough has been said now to plant the suggestion that just as science has evolved its own appropriate method of experimentation and investigation and has made countless discoveries, mainly concerning the external world, just so has Buddhism adopted and developed the techniques of analysis and reasoning, to say nothing of concentration and meditation, to its own purpose of formulating the laws by which the mind operates, to provide the basis for our step by step evolution to the highest states of happiness.

Considering now how cause and effect relationships are interpreted within the Buddhist schools, we find two contradictory views. In the quotation from the *Praise for Dependent-Arising* at the beginning of this chapter Tsong Khapa sets forth the view of dependent-arising that is exclusive to the Consequentialist schools. In contrast, the lower Buddhist schools adopt quite the opposite stance and argue that the fact that something arises in dependence on causes and conditions actually establishes that it *is* inherently existent. The lower schools detect no discrepancy between the appearance of phenomena as inherently existent and their actual mode of existence. When all is said and done, some of them would argue, we can see with our eyes that things are inherently existent. If we refuse to accept our own bare sense perceptions as valid, how can we possibly discriminate between what exists and what does not? We have no choice but to say that our sense perceptions are by and large in direct contact with reality. Things like cups, houses and table which appear to our senses to exist by way of their own independent entities really exist in that way. Certainly such things are created from cause and conditions but could they really exist if they did not have independent entities? Nagarjuna, a great Indian commentator who pioneered the Middle Way School of interpretation and brought what are known as the Great Vehicle or Mahayana teachings into the mainstream of Buddhist practice, sets forth the two opposing views succinctly in his *Treatise on the Middle Way*:

The Lower Schools:

> If all these are empty (of inherent existence),
> There will be no arising and disintegration;
> For you even the four noble truths
> Will become non-existent.

The Consequentialist:

> If all these are not empty (of inherent existence),
> There will be no arising and disintegration;
> For you even the four noble truths
> Will become non-existent.

So the reasoning: The subject, a house, inherently exists because it arises in dependence on causes and conditions, would be a valid argument from the lower school's point of view. A house inherently exists. The bricks and building materials that it is made of inherently exist and the atoms and so forth that make up the building materials also inherently exist. If the parts of the house were not inherently existent, they argue, when you put them together how would you have a house? For example, we may dream about building a house. We may dream that we have the various building materials. However, we obviously cannot build a real house with these dream materials. Why not? Because, as we discover when we awake, such materials were just in the nature of appearance, and not established from their own side. Compare the image of a person projected on to a screen by a film projector with a real person: with respect to these two different appearances of a person, on what basis, asks the proponents of the lower school's views, can the Consequentialist identify which is actually a person and which is not? For the lower schools it is easy. The projected image is not a person but is the mere appearance of a person, because from the side of the object there is no person to be found, as it were, to back up the appearance. The real person is a person because he is established from his own side as such. The Consequentialists' position is that nothing exists from its own side. Therefore they must accept the absurd consequence that, according to their view, there is no valid means to discriminate between the film image of a person and an actual person!

Moreover, if the state of liberation or enlightenment was not established from its own side but was just imputed by the mind, being some kind of mental projection, what reason would there be for attaining such a thing, and what benefit would there be in it? If the I were merely mentally imputed how could we migrate from one life to the next? How could we experience pleasure and pain? If virtue and non-virtue, positive and negative actions were devoid of inherent existence what meaning would there be in engaging in one and abandoning the other? According to this critique by the lower schools then, the error of those who propound no inherent existence is so great that in their system the idea of such a thing as the path to liberation, the distinction between right and wrong and even the distinction between existence and non-existence lose all meaning.

In reply, the Consequentialists themselves admit that if one is a beginner in dharma practice, who doesn't have a very profound understanding of the teachings, then such an exposition as set forth by the lower schools, in which dependent-arising only refers to caused phenomena and is compatible with inherent existence, may well be a suitable basis for engaging in the dharma. Hearing that by practising virtue and abandoning non-virtue we can reach liberation can cause joy in some people and inspire them to take a new and wholesome direction in life. They feel great pleasure as if remembering something wonderful which they had always known but somehow had been temporarily forgotten or overlooked. Hearing nothing in this exposition by someone of the lower schools which contradicts their natural, instinctive assumption that all things inherent exist, then such a type of newcomer to the Buddha's teaching might feel all the more comfortable with their new outlook on life and thereby generate pleasure and enthusiasm in their practice.

The Buddha well understood that his ultimate teaching of no inherent existence would be beyond the range of some of his listeners' thought in the beginning and in view of this he taught the systems presented in the lower schools as lower steps or rungs by which such disciples might eventually reach an understanding of the highest explanation. But it would be mistaken to imagine that anyone can go either all the way to the enlightenment of a Buddha or to the lesser state of liberation from his or her own suffering in dependence on the lower school's view alone. To become free from cyclic existence it is indispensable that we meditate again and again on the ultimate mode of existence of phenomena, their emptiness of inherent existence. Being a subtle phenomena it is not easy to understand. We tend to have much more faith in the gross objects grasped by our senses. We have become very familiar over countless lifetimes with our way of seeing things as existing inherently, from their own side, and we tend to cling to what we are familiar with. Nevertheless, by using the reasoning presented by the highest school of Buddhist thought, the Consequentialists, we will understand that this habitual mode of seeing is wrong and by persevering further we can wipe away the various layers of ignorance that encrust the natural purity of our mind.

IV

Dependent Arising and Emptiness
Two View

The mind of crystal clarity that sees ultimate reality directly is developed through intensive meditation on the reasons which infallibly establish the nature of that reality. How dependent-arising is the chief of these reasons is the subject of this book. This is not to say that Buddhist path to freedom from suffering consists solely in training in reasoning and logic. The complete path has three divisions known as the three higher trainings, in moral discipline, concentration and wisdom. Then again, the type of Buddhism that spread and flourished in Tibet, Great Vehicle Buddhism, emphasizes the practice of compassion and concern for others to an extraordinary degree. However we have no space here to dwell on the teachings on moral discipline, concentration or compassion. Our subject falls into the category of wisdom, which is not surprisingly where effort in reasoning is most needed. If we can develop the compassionate motivation to benefit all sentient beings impartially, that is excellent. In any case, if we can restrain our behaviour according to suitable moral guidelines, our mind will become steadier, less scattered and distracted. This gives us a suitable basis for building up a strong degree of concentration, which, when coupled with our wisdom-understanding will lead to insights. But before we can meditate productively on the ultimate nature of reality, which is indeed the meditation which will free us from the round of uncontrolled existence, we must first form a very clear picture of what it is and how to cultivate it. Arriving at even a clear mental image of it will for most of us require plenty of study, discussion, reflection and a willingness to try to reason things out. To try to proceed by intuition or meditation alone without bothering with these things may only lead to frustration, as in the following examples.

Suppose you have to tell a couple of children, possibly relatives of yours, to go to Moscow or some distant place, let us say to meet their father. Just letting them know that Moscow is in Russia, giving them a good reason for going there and telling them to go will not achieve a great deal. Being young children they have only the slightest idea of where Moscow and Russia are. Still less do they have any idea of how to get there, what documents they require and so forth. If they did set off on their own without any instructions, they would quickly get lost or become discouraged and give up, much as they might actually want to go. So what about someone who, hearing about nirvana or liberation and hearing that people reach nirvana by meditating on no-self and the emptiness of all phenomena, thereupon sits down with eyes closed, meditating with lots of inspiration and joyous enthusiasm...? Is not their quest equally certain to end in discouragement and failure? Or what if someone were given a gun and told to go out and shoot a deer, but that person had no idea what a deer looked like or where he was likely to find one. he might go out and fire his gun at something else. He might even shoot another person! The city of Moscow and the deer of our examples are far more easily recognizable objects than the subtler levels of ignorance that affect our minds. How much more carefully do we need to investigate and analyse therefore when trying to locate and eradicate our ignorance.

The practice of generosity and patience, refraining from harming others and developing compassion are greatly to be treasured. They must be practised by anyone who would imitate the Buddha or other great spiritual teachers, but the Consequentialist master Chandrakirti, highlighting the crucial importance of correctly identifying and vanquishing our root ignorance, call these good qualities 'eyeless.' In the *Supplement to the Middle Way*, he says:

> A single person with sight
> Can easily lead a group of blind people to their destination.
> Similarly a person who has the eyeless good qualities
> Can go to Buddhahood when guided by the wisdom see-
>   ing reality.

Looking more closely now at the views of the Buddhist schools below the Consequentialists, it is not so difficult to understand that caused phenomena or products are dependent-arisings in the sense that they arise in dependence on causes and conditions. A sprout comes forth from a seed. A child comes forth from his or her mother. The production of a sprout involves the coming together of an array of contributory factors. Soil or some similar medium is required in which there is the correct degree of moisture and warmth. If there is too much water the seed will rot; too little and it will remain a seed. For its production it definitely relies on a host of things other than itself. But when we see a sprout once it has been produced, it appears to exist from its own side, it appears to possess its own intrinsic identity. So although it is not self-produced, it nevertheless appears to be self-reliant in the sense of possessing a nature that exists from within itself.

Very few people get round to questioning this appearance of inherent existence. The lower Buddhist schools assent to it. Whatever reservations some of them may have about other aspects of a sprout's mode of appearance, according to them a sprout both appears to exist inherently and does so. The lower schools propound varying degrees of selflessness, some of great refinement, but none of them abandon the idea that the I exists from its own side. Other objects appear to the self as if independent of it, not relying upon the I, but existing in their own right. The lower schools assent to this and do not recognize that self and other depend on each other for their existence. They ask, 'If objects did not have an identity independent of our observation of them, how could they act as a valid basis for our apprehension of them?'

According to them it is not in the basic way in which self and other are apprehended that is at fault; the problems begin when we develop exaggerated reactions to the self-existent I and the self-existent other. We generate a neurotic attachment to the I and cling to it and grasp at possessions, dear ones and allies, while developing impatience and exasperation for those who stand in our way, loathing for our enemies and envy for the possessions of rich and successful.

The fourth and highest school of Buddhist tenets, the Middle Way School, has, as we have said, two divisions, the Autonomists and the Consequentialists. The Autonomists, the lower of the two, put forward a further view of dependent-arising which is more extensive than that of the arising of effects in dependence on causes and embraces all phenomena. The explanation of dependent-arising furnished by the three lower schools is fine as far as it goes but it is incomplete, they say, because it fails to deal with permanent or uncaused phenomena.[6]

According to the Autonomists, if something is not a dependent-arising, then it does not exist. In the case of a table, not only does it depend on its causes, the wood from which it was made and so forth but it, the whole table, depends on its parts. When we perceive a table, the parts of a table, for example the legs, the smooth top, the parts nearer to the eye, the parts further away, the parts in the light and the parts in the shadow, apprehended together, go to make up the apprehension of a table. A person depends on his causes, his mother and father and so forth, and also he depends on his own parts, or characteristics, such as the colour of his skin, the shape of his body, his posture and habitual gestures, in the sense that only when someone apprehends sufficient of these features together are they able to apprehend him and discriminate him from anybody else.

Notice the shift in emphasis in this second explanation of dependent-arising away from the status of objects in their own right to a recognition of the interrelation of objects and subjects. This is a trend that we will find taken significantly further by the Consequentialists. The Autonomists still hold parts and whole to exist from their own side and to exist by way of their own characteristics however. With respect to the mode of being of phenomena, the Autonomists special position is that they assert a mode of being which is established from the object's own side, but which is posited through the power of appearing to a non-defective awareness. Their principal explanation of how phenomena are selfless therefore is that they are empty of existing from their own side without depending on being posited by a non-defective awareness. This is another way in which their view shows an advance in refinement over the lower schools. We may like to ask ourselves, for instance, whether the Autonomist views provides a better basis for explaining how different people see the same thing in slightly different ways.

From the highest point of view, that of the Consequentialists, the above explanation do not reveal the full import of the reasoning of dependent-arising. Properly understood, the reason of dependent-arising refutes any shadow of the existence of objects from their own side whatsoever. But it is very difficult to jump to the subtler explanations of dependent-arising straight away and one purpose of our introductory exploration of the other schools is to enable us first to focus precisely on just what the Consequentialists use the reasoning of dependent-arising to destroy—our instinctive assent to and grasping at the appearance of all and any phenomena to us as inherently existing, as having a mode of subsistence from the side of the object. If we think about and discuss the views of the other schools and then meditate on them and try to bring them within the realm of our own experience we will find that, while some of the various assertions of the different schools contradict each other, they all in the end contribute most helpfully towards shedding light on this instinctive, subtlest, most tenacious and most harmful ignorance of all.

A term which crops up frequently in debates between the schools about the precise nature of the ignorance that is the source of all the other delusions and just what antidote will eradicate it, is true existence. We have avoided using it much so far because it is one of those terms which different schools interpret in different ways, but thinking about it will give another slant to our understanding of what the Consequentialists single out as the key object of refutation. According to the Consequentialist interpretation, inherent existence, existence from the side of the object and true existence are all synonymous, so that for the Consequentialists nothing truly exists, which is by no means the same as saying that nothing is true and that everything is false, as we shall attempt to explain. We can approach the problem first by considering the term false. Three different usages of the term false can be distinguished. The first is the way the word is most commonly used in the world. If someone accuses us of stealing something when we have done nothing of the kind, then the statement of the other person is obviously false. Or our senses may be deceived, for instance when we are sitting in a stationary train but have the distinct impression that it is moving, only to realize a few second later that it is another train which we can see out of the window that is in fact moving and our train has not moved at all. We can say the consciousness we had for those few seconds was a false consciousness.

The second meaning of false that we can distinguish concerns what is false according to someone's tenets or beliefs. Having studied a particular political, religious or scientific system and adopted it, one judges something to be false according to that framework, for instance, someone who is a holder of Buddhist views would regard the opinion that the mind is a material phenomenon as false. The third usage of the word false is the one closely connected with the Buddhist presentation of the ultimate nature of phenomena and occurs in the phrase "falsely existent". All phenomena appear to an ordinary consciousness to exist from their own side, but when investigated are found to have no such mode of existence whatsoever. For this reason, according to the Consequentialists, all phenomena are falsely existent and therefore non-truly existent. They are so not because they don't exist, but because they do not exist in the way they appear to our ordinary consciousness. In our first usage of the word false, some phenomena are false, such as the water of a mirage which is not water at all, and some are true, such as water, but all phenomena—even those which are true in the first sense—are falsely existent. So a holder of the Consequentialist point of view can assert that no phenomenon truly or inherently exists but within that still discriminate between water that really is wet and water that is merely a mirage on a hot day. The Autonomists and Mind-Only followers have somewhat different notions of exactly what discrepancy between appearance and actuality the words non-truly existent should denote, but we will not venture into that here.

That phenomena depend on conditions is sufficient to establish for the Consequentialists, Tsong Khapa included, that they are empty of inherent existence. The lower schools disagree and hold completely the opposite view, that anything which depends on causes and conditions is necessarily inherently existent. We have sketched in the points of view of some of the lower schools and have tried to give the reasons why they think as they do. Ideally we should first try to see things in the way that the lower schools do. In that way their flaws, the areas in which their explanations leave us feeling dissatisfied, might become apparent to us. If we reach this point, then we will be in a position to readily absorb the Consequentialist view, and those who do directly understand that phenomena both arise in dependence upon conditions and are thereby empty of true existence are said to develop a sublime kind of joy and a profound faith in the teacher Buddha, since they thereby penetrate to the very essence of the teachings and generate the actual path to freedom. Those fortunate ones who gain this direct realization glorify Buddha and his teaching although few have done it as eloquently as Tsong Khapa.

The data we begin with is again that all objects appear to have their own intrinsic identity residing within the object or from the side of the object. All objects appear to exist by way of their own intrinsic nature. Water's nature is to be wet with the power of moistening. Fire's nature is to be hot with the power of burning. But if water and fire had those characteristics from their own side then this means that they would not depend on any other phenomena for those characteristics. This would mean that any particular fire could never go out. If its hot and burning nature were independent of any other phenomena then what could act to extinguish it and how could it ever die out for lack of fuel? If a seed and a sprout were both established inherently, with their own intrinsic natures then the sprout would not arise in dependence on the seed and the seed would not produce it. Yet what meaning does the word seed have? A seed is something which has the capacity to produce a sprout. But if the entities of the seed and the sprout each existed from their own side, through their own power, then they would be unrelated. A seed's nature could not transform into the nature of a sprout. Another synonym for existence from the side of the object and inherent existence, according to the Consequentialists, is existence by way of the object's own characteristics. If we do not understand this term properly, like the term non-truly existent, it could lead us astray. We are not suggesting that a sprout and fire have no characteristics or nature of their own. What we mean is that these characteristics are not intrinsic to those objects, because then the fault would arise that since these characteristics would be independent of any affecting factors, the object would neither gain nor lose characteristics and could never transform into anything else or cease to exist.

When we set about meditating and trying to uproot our instinctive grasping at inherent existence, the most important object to dwell on is the I. If we consider how we ordinarily grasp at the I, we tend to apprehend it as a very solid, independent phenomena that is able to set itself up from its own side. This is especially apparent if we observe the I when we are in a state of strong emotion such as anger, fear, desire, or happiness. This is the best time to check up on the false mode of appearance of the I, when we are strongly moved. But if the I were really an independent object, then it could not be said to depend on the mind or body for its existence. So then, if we had a pain in our body, in our arm for example, there would be no reason to say, 'I have a pain.' But if someone asked us, 'Are you experiencing pain?' then could we not correctly answer, 'Yes,' and pointing to our arm say, 'I am experiencing pain in my arm?' Are these statements false, or do they reveal a dependent relationship between the I and the body? Surely the I cannot be separated from and therefore depends on its parts, the mind and body. The mind is not the I and the body is not the I. The I depends on for its identity on things which are not it, so the assertions of the lower schools that it has an intrinsic identity or that it exists inherently cannot be substantiated.

In another sense the I is dependent because it depends on others. In order to distinguish the I, we have to distinguish it *from others*. If we are to identify one object as self, we have, at the same time, to establish another category, other or others, for the term self to have any meaning. It is the same with the terms here and there. The place where we are now, we call here, but if there is no place to call there to contrast it with, how could the term be understood? Furthermore, to a person on the other side of the room, or road, or valley or whatever, from their point of view, where they are located is here and where we are is there. So for one particular place there are two different apprehensions, one valid for each of the two observers. Neither place is intrinsically here or there. The 'hereness' or 'thereness' is clearly not established from the side of object. Hot and cold, beautiful and ugly, pleasant and unpleasant and generality and particular are similar pairs of terms which are mutually dependent. None of the individual terms have an identity in their own right, or are able to set themselves up from their own side.

We have briefly mentioned three ways in which the I or the self is a dependent phenomena. It depends on its parts, it depends on others and it depends on the point of view of who is using the term. If we could devote time to any one of these modes of dependent-arising of the self and cause the strength of our habitual misapprehension of the self as autonomous and as established by way of its own characteristics to subside, at least to some extent, it would be very beneficial. We are not attempting to get rid of a sense of I, only of the idea of this I as self-existent or as established from its own side. Why should we try to get rid of the idea of the I as self-existent and established from its own side? Because this is a false notion that obscures what is really the case and when we act on the basis of a misunderstanding we are likely to act unskillfully and end up causing problems for ourself and others. For instance, if we think we know a particular subject very well and develop pride in our knowledge, or even if we have a handsome and expensive house or car and we become proud about that and swagger about it, people are going to find it somewhat harder to like us. But then if we think more realistically about our level of knowledge or the quality of our house or car and compare ourselves not just with those people who are less well off than us in this or that respect, but also with the many who are far better off—much more knowledgeable, or possessing a really fabulous house or car—then our pride will decrease and people will find us less obnoxious, though of course our knowledge will not have decreased or will the value of our house or car have gone down. Similarly, thinking more realistically about how the self exists, in the way the Consequentialists propose, will not cause our sense of self to disappear but simply align it better with reality. This will bestow peace of mind, which is the object of the exercise.

The term conditions in the first line of the fifth verse, 'Whatever depends on causes and conditions,' is another term which is used differently by the lower schools and the Consequentialists. To the lower schools a condition is similar to a cause. Causes and conditions are what produce caused or impermanent phenomena such as consciousness, trees and mountains. The main object or objects which transform into a particular thing can be thought of as the cause of that result while the other contributory factors which may arise only just prior to the formation of the effect can be thought of as the conditions. For instance, in Tibetan medicine there is a category of illnesses which are of a hot nature and a category of those which are of a cold nature. When someone who has a complaint of a cold nature goes out in cold weather the illness manifests and they start to feel unwell. The illness itself is something which has a causal sequence beginning well before the present occasion. The cold weather is on the other hand the temporary condition which causes the symptoms to manifest strongly so that the person feels indisposed. The Consequentialists, however, also say that it is not only caused or impermanent phenomena that arise in dependence on conditions. The dependent relationship we mentioned earlier between here and there, generality and particular, beautiful and ugly, part and part-possessor and so forth are such that these phenomena are also said to arise in dependence upon conditions, without their necessarily being products or impermanent phenomena. Also all phenomena, both those which are produced and those which are not, have conception as one of the conditions for their establishment. For example, someone decides to make a vase for holding flowers in. First of all they hold a concept of the vase in their mind, that is they have a mental picture of the vase they want to create in their mind's eye. Then they actually go about to manufacture the vase. When it is finished, it is given the name, a vase. This name is applied to it by a conceptual mind to distinguish it from other objects. Take America as another example. Before westerners arrived there was obviously land there, but only after they arrived was the land named America, and not until the concept of America was formulated and the name America applied could anyone know what America was. All phenomena are designated by conception and so conception is one of the conditions of any phenomenon's establishment. Thus the Consequentialists hold that 'Whatever depends on conditions...' refers to all phenomena in that all phenomena are established in dependence on conditions. However, not all phenomena are *created* in dependence upon conditions. That only applies to impermanent phenomena.

In summary, when we apprehend an object such as a table, we apprehend an object that is produced in dependence on an infinite series of causes whose many different parts, the colour, the shape, the top, the sides, the legs and so forth, go to make up our apprehension of it, but the way a table appears to us, whether we look directly at one whether we close our eyes and think about one, is that it appears to have a nature which exists from its own side; this is a sense of 'tableness' appearing to reside right there within the object. When an object appears to set itself up like this, appearing not to depend on any other phenomena, the apprehension we have at that time is an apprehension of a truly existent, or an inherently existent object, that exists from its own side, by way of its own characteristics. Conversely, when we see a phenomena and clearly understand that the very existence of it is completely dependent on other phenomena, inseparably related to them, then at that time our mind is holding the view of dependent-arising. The basis for the apprehension of things as truly existent does not exist. There is no phenomenon which exists independently of others. The basis for the apprehension of things as dependent-arisings does exist. The only way phenomena do exist is as interdependently related. Obviously then, despite what the lower schools think, we cannot on the one hand accept inherent existence and also accept that phenomena inter-depend and, in the case of impermanent phenomena, cause each other. These two ways of existing are plainly contradictory.

5-cd What excellent instruction could there be
       More amazing than these words?

...especially for someone who has followed the teachings of the lower schools and developed completely the opposite view! But for anybody, it is stressed, to realize the full import of dependent-arising, namely that all phenomena are empty of inherent existence, is an extremely forceful experience that reorients one in the very depths of one's being, cancels doubts and wrong views and bestows peace.

V

Dependent-Arising and Emptiness
The Final View

6. Through wrongly holding (dependent-arising),
    The childish strengthen bondage to extreme views.
    But for the wise, the same thing is the means
    To cut free from the net of elaborations.

In the first line of the sixth verse, those who wrongly hold or apprehend dependent-arising are all those who have not attained to the
highest Consequentialist view of it and although all Buddhists would
agree that Buddha taught a middle way, free from extremes, the highest
Buddhist school, of which the Consequentialists are a sub-group, in
particular characterize themselves as maintaining the true middle
course, free from 'bondage to extreme views,' so much so that, as we
may recall, they are named the Middle Way School. The extreme
views are basically two. One is the abyss of nihilism. The unfortunates
who plunge to this extreme are those who search through the aggregates
of body and mind and like the Consequentialists come up with
nothing substantial that they can point at and identify as the self.
They then, unlike the Consequentialists, take it that the self does not
exist and assume that the myriad objects of knowledge are also merely
mistaken appearances, *maya,* or illusion. Life for them becomes a
meaningless game, devoid of any high purpose, with no distinction
possible between good and bad or truth and falsehood, at best an
exercise in keeping the upper lip stiff.

   The other extreme is the abyss of permanence. Those who plunge
to this extreme identify something either amongst the aggregates of
body and mind or apart from them as an inherently existing I, grasp
strongly at a fixed essence to the person and possibly also at an

unchanging essence in objects that endures throughout all the superficial changes in their outward semblance. Such a strong grasping at
an inherently existent I and 'mine' is the ideal basis for the poisonous
delusions of desirous attachment and aversion to come springing forth.
These delusions in turn motivate negative actions and thus the
perpetuation of cyclic existence is assured. 'The wise,' on the other
hand, use the reasoning of dependent-arising to steer away from the
abysses of nihilism and permanence and arrive at the correct and
liberating view of phenomena as empty of inherent existence. In
another image, understanding dependent-arising will enable us to
cut through the 'net of elaborations.' Elaborations are the countless
misconceptions generated by the mistaken appearances of reality that
all sentient beings have. The mistaken appearance above all is that of
inherent existence of course and under its influence many paths,
supposedly to complete happiness but merely leading up many cul-
de-sacs to only limited partial happiness, have been explained. We
have mentioned some of these alternatives above. There is the path of
absolute inaction by which the practitioner thinks to attain liberation
by exhausting all his or her previous karma without accumulating
any fresh actions. There is the method of mental vacuity practised by
those who see thought as the root of all problems and try to gain
liberation by focussing the mind on nothingness in meditation. There
are also in India practitioners who engage in various forms of physical
endurance of pain, fasting and asceticism in the belief this will bring
about an end to their negative karma and thus lead to freedom from
suffering. Buddha himself spent six years in an experiment with
asceticism before rejecting it as a path to liberation. Buddhism also
stands apart from those religions the practice of which is largely
devotional, validated by revealed truth alone, for we contend that
final happiness comes about through understanding and that understanding can be achieved through the application of reason. So also
to those who picture the world as an endless maze without a middle
course, or as a fundamentally random jumble of events, in other words
to those who feel that the net of fabrications can never be ripped
apart, we say, in the words of the Middle Way master Aryadeva in his
treatise *The Four Hundred,*

When dependent-arising is seen,
Ignorance is not generated.
Insight into the selfless nature of phenomena
Destroys the seed of cyclic existence.

In order to try to understand the subtlest explanation of the root ignorance, as delineated by the Consequentialists, we have sketched in the helpful, though incomplete, explanations of the lower schools concerning the mode of existence of phenomena in general. The lower schools also have their own special explanations of this root ignorance specifically in terms of the I or self. Ignorance concerning the I is generally recognised as the most pernicious kind of ignorance because it is primarily due to misconceiving the nature of the I that the disturbing attitudes of clinging attachment, jealousy, anger and pride come about. If we understand the Consequentialist point of view well, we shall see that there is, in fact, no difference between the kind of ignorance that obscures our view of the self and the kind of ignorance that obscures our view of other phenomena. In both cases it is the ignorance which superimposes the appearance of inherent existence on to the object. In the lower schools on the other hand distinctions are drawn between the ignorance regarding the elf and the ignorance regarding other phenomena, so two different kinds of ignorance are described in each of these schools. Here we will merely pick out the two main misconceptions of the I that the lower schools say must be eradicated in order to gain liberation and contrast them with what the Consequentialists say is the root ignorance that binds us to the wheel of existence.

The first wrong conception of the I that the lower schools refute is the apprehension of the I as permanent, single and independent. This is an I which is permanent because it is without production and disintegration, single in the sense that is it without parts and independent because it does not depend on the aggregates or anything else. It is like a pea in a jar, the jar being the aggregates of body and mind and the pea being the I residing within the aggregates until the aggregates disintegrate at death, at which point the I goes on to its next rebirth. The second misconception of the I is grasping the I to be the substantially established in the sense of being self-sufficient.

This misapprehension is subtler than the former and is held to be the main obstacle to individual liberation by the schools below the Consequentialists. It is the conception of the existence of a self which is capable of being identified independently, without relying on the identification of the aggregates. The feeling one has when grasping at this I is of there being something to which all the aggregates belong, and owner or governor of them, something which has a different character to them and possesses them, thinking, 'Mine.'

According to the Consequentialists, while it is necessary to abandon these two levels of ignorance, that alone is not sufficient to cut free of the net of elaborations concerning the self. To do that we need to abandon not just these two gross levels of self-grasping but also the subtler level of grasping at the self to be inherently existent. To refute the first false notion of the I we would do well to consider why the I must be impermanent. Our bodies and our minds are changing from moment to moment. Both a person and the parts of that person are effects and at the same time causes involved in a continual process of transformation. Is there any place for a permanent, i.e., unchanging I or self in all this? With regard to the second false apprehension of I we have to break down our instinctive grasping at an independently identifiable I, controlling the aggregates, but not relying on them. To counter this attitude we have to investigate how the apprehension of the self always depends on apprehending some other phenomena. We recognize somebody only by apprehending some part of them, their face or general shape, perhaps. If it is somebody we know very well we can recognize them just by hearing their cough or the sound of their footsteps. However the self exists, it does not exist over and above the aggregates, but is inseparable from them. The subtlest self grasping, grasping the self to be inherently existent, is countered by applying arguments to establish that a self existing either from the side of the aggregates or separate from them is completely unfindable. We have to mentally search again and again through the parts of the self, all through the body and the mind, to convince ourselves no one part is the self, anymore than we can isolate one part of a telephone from the rest of the parts and say "That is the telephone." Our body is not the self. If it was, how could we say, "I am thinking?" Our mental consciousness is not the self. Otherwise how could we say,

"Somebody touched me" or "I kicked the ball?" Although it is completely contrary to the way we normally apprehend ourselves, reasoning shows that among the parts of the mind and body there is nothing that we can point to and say, "This is the I." We should extend the search for the I outside the aggregates to convince ourselves that there is no I which exists completely separate from its parts either. The next stage is to familiarize ourselves deeply with the absence of an I that exists by way of its own entity, by going over this reasoning again and again, and gradually our habitual self-grasping will lose its power.[7]

Finally, one telling difference between the lower schools and the Consequentialists is that the former all agree that, after removing the superimpositions or false appearances of the self, the actual I can be identified within the aggregates and, as it were, pointed out. To take one example, the Autonomists, the other followers of the Middle Way School, apart from the Consequentialists, point to some form of the mental consciousness as the I. The Consequentialists, on the other hand, refute any suggestion that the actual I can be found within the aggregates and only speak of an I which is designated to its basis of designation, the parts of the I, by the conceptual mind.

7.   Since this teaching is not found elsewhere,
     You alone are the 'Teacher.'
     For a tirthika, this name would be a flattery,
     Like calling a fox a lion.

8.   O wondrous teacher! O wondrous refuge!
     Supreme speaker! Great Protector!
     I pay homage to the Great Teacher
     Who so clearly explained dependent-arising.

In the first line of the seventh verse 'teaching' refers to the teaching of emptiness of inherent existence of all phenomena by the reason of dependent-arising. 'This teaching is not found elsewhere' asserts that it is unique to the Buddhist canon. Furthermore, it is only distinguished in the commentaries of Consequentialists, being overlooked by the philosophers even of the other Buddhist schools. 'Tirthika' was the Sanskrit term employed by Buddhist writers for the followers of other non-Buddhist Indian philosophical schools. One way of explaining the four epithets for the Buddha in the eighth verse is to say that 'wondrous teacher' refers to the Buddha as the teacher of the lower schools tenets, where he did not deny inherent existence, and 'wondrous refuge' is a praise to the Buddha for teaching the highest system of tenets in which the inseparability of emptiness and dependent-arising is revealed. Understanding this is our ultimate refuge from the suffering of cyclic existence. 'Supreme speaker' refers to the Buddha's teaching of the lower schools' view again, in accordance with the needs of those of lesser capacity and 'Great Protector' is again a description merited by the Buddha's ultimate teaching on dependent-arising and emptiness for the students of great capacity. This verse, the eighth, is called the homage of the main text whereas the first verse was the homage of the introduction.

9.   O Benefactor! To heal all beings
      You proclaimed (dependent-arising),
      The peerless reason for ascertaining
      Emptiness, the heart of the teaching.

10.   How could those who see
      The way of profound dependent-arising
      As contradictory or unproven
      Ever understand your system?

That which destroys cyclic existence from the root is the meditation on the emptiness of inherent existence of the self and phenomena. Dependent-arising is the peerless reasoning for understanding it. Sometimes dependent-arising is called, 'The King of Reasonings.' The non-Buddhist philosophical schools, for example the Hindu schools of India, are the ones who, when presented with a reasoning such as: 'Considering the subject, the self; it is empty of inherent existence because it is a dependent-arising,' would be most likely to reply that the reason in the above syllogism, 'because it is a dependent-arising' was not proven. The lower Buddhist schools are the ones who would most probably answer by saying that the reason was contradictory, since for them something's being a dependent-arising is a sign that it is inherent existent. We mentioned some of the lower schools counter arguments in chapter III, using the examples of the film image of a man and a house seen in a dream. We can now try to answer these objections, though first we will restate them with a couple of more illustrations. The first is when someone sees a length of rope in the grass at dusk and panics, thinking he or she is about to tread on a snake. Clearly the thing lurking in the grass from its own side is not a snake. There is merely somebody imputing a snake in that place. Consequentialists have to admit that a real snake is very similar to the imaginary snake in this situation because they hold the real snake also to be merely imputed, lacking an identity as a snake from the side of the object. Therefore does not the Consequentialist have to accept the absurdity that, according to his own tenets, the imaginary snake is a real snake since he has no valid means to discriminate between them? Compare dream experiences with experiences of the waking state: since both sets of experiences are merely projected by the mind and have no true existence, no distinction can be drawn between them in terms of whether the experiences are actual or not. If, for example, a fully ordained monk (who has strict vows against killing) dreamed that he deliberately murdered someone and rejoiced in having done so, would not he have broken his vows? In his dream he only killed a person who was merely imputed, but so what? The Consequentialists would have you believe that even a person whom you might kill during the waking state has no mode of existence other than as a mere imputation by conception.

In fact these questions were posed quite some time ago. The question about killing in a dream is recorded in sutra as having been asked of the Buddha himself, while the question about the rope and the snake was dealt with by Nagarjuna, the great Indian commentator. Unfortunately this does not mean that it is possible to formulate the answers very simply. When the lower school debaters hear the Consequentialists say that all phenomena are merely imputations, they assume that this signifies that all phenomena are merely imaginary. They say that to call something a mere imputation denies the existence of any object at all except for some conjured up figment of the imagination. The Consequentialists are only denying that objects exist by way of their own characteristics which of course to them is very different from denying objects altogether. So Consequentialists say in reply that when we impute an object it is certainly necessary to have a valid basis for such an imputation. A rope for instance is not a valid basis on which to impute a snake.

The lower schools, on their part, say that a piece of rope is not a snake simply because it is not a snake from its own side, and that a real snake is a snake because it is a snake from its own side. This explanation fails to acknowledge the exclusive role of imputation in conceiving and identifying objects. In order to demonstrate how a phenomenon can be *merely* imputed by the mind apprehending it, consider the following example: suppose somebody produces a superb forgery of a hundred rupee note, so good that only the most experienced experts at the national mint can tell the difference between it and the real thing. In quality of paper, engraving and colouring the fake is virtually identical with an actual one hundred rupee note; only one or two minute details distinguish it. Of these virtually identical scraps of paper, how does one come to be worth one hundred rupees, while the other fit only to be shredded? It is simply because the experts, with the backing of the legal system, pronounce one to be real money, having that face value and pronounce the other to be worthless. Purely through the force of imputation then, one piece of paper is exchangeable for a hundred rupees worth of goods while the other has no value. In the case of a snake, someone at a certain time in the past first gave the name snake to a certain object, the animal with the characteristics unique to snakes. To the basis they applied the designation 'snake.' Just so today, when enough of those characteristics, the sinuous body, the absence of legs, the patterned skin, the fangs and so on, appear to mind, we may validly impute snake to that set of characteristics. In our example of a length of a rope lying on the ground in the twilight, on the basis of an appearance to mind of a sinuous, legless animal with poison fangs lurking in the grass, the person walking in the dusk apprehends snake and recoils in horror. But if he takes a close look at the object in the grass, although he will see a sinuous legless form, he will see nothing he could call a body or a possessor of fangs, nothing he could call a head or tail, nothing he could call an animal even. So a closer examination of the basis of imputation, the rope, reveals that it is not something to which one can ascribe the uncommon characteristics of a snake and therefore it is unsuitable to apprehend it as a snake. There are two significant differences between the mind which apprehends an actual snake and one that apprehends a rope as a snake. Firstly, we cannot ascribe to the rope the qualities of having a body or fangs or a forked tongue or the qualities of being able to crawl on its belly along the ground or to bite other creatures. Therefore it is not a fit basis for the designation snake. Secondly, if the person who originally thought the rope was a snake takes a second, closer, look then he will be able to see that the rope is not a snake but a rope. This latter perception, of a rope lying in the grass, is a correct or valid perception and it establishes that the former perception, of the rope as a snake, was mistaken. It is capable of overturning the former perception; in other words the former perception can be disproven. Therefore a rope is not a basis for the designation, snake.

If we are asked whether the object designated, the snake, resides within the basis of designation, the characteristics or parts, we have to answer that indeed it does not. For instance, the skin of the snake is not the snake; the long thin body is not the snake; nor are the fangs, nor any of the other features either individually or collectively. The fact is that a conceptual mind apprehends a snake by imputing it on to a number of characteristics which appear to that mind, none of which are themselves a snake. People who say that a snake exists by way of its own entity or from its own side are obliged to come up with something among the parts, features or characteristics of a snake that it essentially the snake. Unless they are able to put forward something substantial like that to point at as the actual object or at least a substantial basis on which to hang their imputation, they have to acknowledge that the snake is merely imputed. In the case of sentient beings, most of the lower schools posit the mental consciousness in one form or another as this substantial factor which is the inherent essence of that being. In the case of inanimate objects it is somewhat harder to point to any individual feature as the essence of the object. The two lowest schools, The Particularists and the Sutra-followers, say at this point that, in the case of inanimate objects, the collection of the parts of the object is the object. For instance, the collection of the parts of a motor car is a motor car. To this the Consequentialists respond, "If all the parts of a car were dumped anyhow in a heap in front of you, the collection of parts would be there but they would not cause you to think, 'That is a car.' Therefore it is incorrect to say that the collection of the parts of a car is a car." The followers of

Mind Only and the Autonomists on their part put forward the distinctive shape or arrangement of the parts of the object as the object. To them the Consequentialists respond, "Where is this distinctive shape or arrangement of parts of the car? No individual part possesses it. Instead of existing from the side of the parts, is not this distinctive shape or arrangement of parts something designated to them when they are assembled?" This is contrary with the car's supposed findability or ability to be located within the object. Thus this shape or arrangement of parts does not fulfill the criterion of being something which, from its own side, is the car.

Consider the person who made the first car. First he had a concept of what he wanted to invent. Then he set about making it. After a few prototypes perhaps, he finally made something which fulfilled his concept. It was able to perform the function of the object he had in mind in the way intended. At this point he designated what he had made as car. All the other cars that have come into the world since then are apprehended in the same way. On the basis of an appearance to mind of the assembled components that are able to perform that particular function the mind imputes, car. What can we say of the ultimate nature of a car other than that it is devoid of any existence from its own side, in the first place because it depends on causes and conditions, in the second place because it depends on its parts and in the third place because it depends on the three, a base of designation, a conceptual mind which designates it and a term to designate it by?

The second problem posed by the advocates of lower school views who are looking for weaknesses in the Consequentialist position concerns the monk who kills someone in a dream. All the schools can agree that the dream victim is not real person because he does not possess the defining characteristics of a person. From the lower schools point of view he does not possess the defining characteristics of a person first and foremost because he is not a person who exists from his own side; this is because he is merely an appearance in somebody's dream. From the Consequentialists' point of view real people do not exist from their own side any more than the ones who appear in dreams. But from their perspective the dream victim does not possess the defining characteristics of a person because, however real he appears to the dreamer during the short time of the dream state, he is not someone who has the ability to speak, to think for himself, to accumulate karma and so on. A real person has to have a certain history too. A real person is born at a certain time in a certain place. It is to some such variety of characteristics as these, embodied only by a person, that the term person or human is suitable to be applied. If the term human or person is applied to any other base of designation such as a figment of imagination in a dream, the film image of a person or the reflection of a person in a mirror then the term is being used incorrectly. From the point of view of their not existing from their own side the real person and the dream person are the same. From the point of view of the way ordinary objects are understood and the way terminology is conventionally used, there is all the difference in the world.

Thus the monk in the example does not accumulate the negative action of killing a person. It is said that some negative karma of a lesser kind may be accumulated due to the generation of the intention to kill in a dream. Generally dreams are a reflection of the actions, mental or physical that one has engaged in during the waking state. Imprints from these actions can manifest during the time of sleep. If one has engaged in very negative actions, this can be reflected in nightmares, while it is said that if one has performed many virtuous actions one will have pleasant dreams. There is another type of dream, which is much less common, when the mind becomes very clear and events that are yet to occur are revealed to us. Sometimes also in a dream we can receive an indication or confirmation that a spirit or evil influence is trying to harm us. There might be other occasions when, if one has a particular strong affinity with one's own meditational deity, this deity can reveal certain things and bestow blessings during a dream. There is also a yogic practice where the adept can use the mind which manifests at the time of sleep. One characteristic of the mind of sleep is that it is, like the mind at the point of death, subtler than the ordinary gross waking consciousness. If one uses this level of consciousness to meditate on certain objects, this can bring about realisations. Here we are talking about somebody with a highly developed mind. Apart from these special cases the majority of dreams are said to arise from the awakening of the latent impressions left by the actions we are most familiar with.

VI

In Daily Life

11.   When one perceives 'empty'
      As the meaning of 'dependent-arising,'
      Empty of inherent existence does not contradict
      The function of agent and action.

12.   Whereas if one perceives the opposite,
      Since there can be neither action in emptiness
      Nor emptiness in what has action,
      One would fall into a dreadful abyss.

13.   Therefore, understanding dependent-arising,
      As you have taught, is well praised.
      (Things) are not totally non-existent,
      Nor are they inherently existent.

14.   The independent is like a sky-flower,
      Therefore nothing is not dependent.
      Existence with self-nature precludes
      Establishment by causes and conditions.

Others see the reasoning of dependent-arising as unproven, or contradictory with that which it is designed to prove, namely that all phenomena are empty of inherent existence. Tsong Khapa relied on the interpretations of the Consequentialist school and realised that emptiness and dependent-arising are supremely harmonious. With this realisation, all his perplexities concerning the ultimate import of Buddha's teaching were dissolved. Perceiving that emptiness of inherent existence and dependent-arising are completely compatible is the incomparable insight of those who actualize the Buddha's highest teachings and is the deepest well-spring of their faith. We can deepen and extend our appreciation of the various facets of dependent-arising by considering it under three headings, depending, relying and meeting or connecting. Even if we feel we are a long way from achieving Tsong Khapa's level of illumination and insight, contemplating these different aspects of dependent-arising is a sure way to develop our good qualities of generosity, tolerance and concern for others.

The first of the three aspects, depending, embraces the simplest level of dependent-arising, that of effects being the product of causes. Considering how effects are dependent on causes is in itself a great antidote to self-centered and self-satisfied attitudes which lead to our being insensitive to the predicament of others and dismissive of the complexity of their problems. When we are doing fine we do not notice how the kindness of many other beings has contributed to our happiness. When we are down we lunge for a simplistic explanation which places all the blame on others. For instance we probably all have the tendency to think that whatever good health we have to a large extent comes about through our own vigilance and whatever experiences we enjoy are the deserved fruits of our own hard work. Our analysis of how the good conditions we enjoy arise often tends to go no further than some such though as 'I know how to take care of myself,' or 'I put in a lot of effort to be able to afford this.' If we go to a restaurant and have a delicious meal, superficially we might think that being able to do this just depends on our own means, having earned enough money to pay for it. However, if we investigate exactly what being able to eat a meal in a restaurant really depends on, we will see that in fact an enormous amount of effort has to be put in by countless number of beings before we can be served our choice of food. If we are eating rice, we can think of all the work of the farmers, ploughing, planting, weeding, irrigating and finally harvesting their crops. Of course all the labour of themselves and their draught animals would be in vain if the elements did not cooperate and provide the right amount of sunshine and rain. Then the rice has to be cleaned and milled and prepared for the table. Then it is distributed and put on sale in the shops. Another network of people is required there. Once the rice has reached the restaurant, the kitchen staff have to work hard on the final stage of the process of making it fit to eat. The kitchen and the dining room themselves are the fruits of the labour of gangs of people and the cook's utensils, the fuel for cooking and the serving dishes have only come into being in dependence on the inventiveness, ingenuity and effort of another vast number of designers, administrators, sales people, accountants, factory workers, miners and then all their families and teachers and so forth.

In Mcleod Ganj, where His Holiness the Dalai Lama lives, there are a considerable number of restaurants catering largely to the westerners and other visitors who come on pilgrimage, to study or just as tourists. As the number of the visitors has increased so have the hotel and restaurant facilities expanded. Clearly the visitors depend on the restaurants and hotels and equally the hotel and restaurant workers depend on the visitors. As the range of facilities for visitors improves, so are more people tempted to come, and as the number of visitors increases, so do more people take to the business of selling them food, souvenirs, handicrafts and books on Buddhism. Many of the Tibetan shop and hotel owners would say that this situation ultimately rests on the kindness of His Holiness and the Three Jewels.[8] They are very happy to see the visitors from other parts of India and the rest of the world who come to Mcleod Ganj, happy on their own account and also when they think of the benefit the visitors can derive from finding out about Buddhism. The visitors are pleased that facilities in McLeod Ganj are not so bad, and that they can get decent food there. They can appreciate the welcome they get and the cheerfulness of the Tibetans and they too can understand that there is mutual benefit for themselves and the Tibetans in their being there. But if either side were to lapse into a more self-centred way of thinking, such as "I am the one who built up this restaurant by my own hard work," or "I can eat at this expensive restaurant because I worked hard and saved up a lot of money," then, thinking that their fortunate situation did not depend on others, only on themselves, there would be a degeneration of this happy feeling between the two sides and the mutual tolerance of each others' foibles.

Another example of the benefits of remembering dependent-arising occurs in the following story about a man who was going to market with a yak. As he was leading the yak along a mountain path the yak slipped and fell off the track. It fell into a narrow place in such a way that it was unable to rise again. So the man made a very strong prayer to the Buddhas, and to Padmasambhava in particular, and by heaving on the rope he was able to get the yak back on its feet. But instead of thinking about the kindness of the Buddhas or the Three Jewels, he set off again on his journey with a very inflated view of his own strength. A little further on the yak fell down again. This time the man thought he could get the yak back to its feet just by tugging on the rope, without bothering with the prayer, but try as he might the yak remained stuck and he could not shift it an inch! Whatever we undertake, if we remember that our success depends on far more than just our own prowess or wealth we will only be more in touch with the reality of the situation, since the dependent relationships of one phenomena with others are in fact countless. Being more in touch with the reality of our situation can only help us—in getting on better with other people for instance. As for the power of prayer, Padmasambhava was one of the first and greatest yogis to spread Buddha's teachings in Tibet and a prayer backed up by strong faith in him can help good karma to ripen at a certain point to bring about a desired result. Just as a child's willingness to learn makes it possible for the teacher to draw out the child's understanding, so, as in the story, making a prayer can help to draw out our ability to solve a particular problem at a critical time.

The second aspect of dependent-arising, relying, does not exclude the relationship between effects and causes we have discussed under the heading dependent, but also stressed in an explanation of relying is the mutual relationship between parts and wholes. We cannot have an apprehension of a table unless we apprehend some of the parts of a table and we cannot understand what a part of a table, such as a table leg or the colour of a table, is without understanding a table. If we are standing outside at night and we see a pair of lights flickering in the distance and then we hear the roar of a motor, we think, "There is a car coming." Simultaneous with the apprehension of a car is the understanding that the lights are the lights of a car and that the engine noise is the noise of a car. A car and the parts of a car, in this instance, its lights and its sound, rely upon each other. Neither is apprehended without the other. Another dimension of the concept of relying is the way in which pairs of things like self and other, short and tall, here and there and subject and object are mutually reliant. The only way self, for instance, can be distinguished is by contrasting it with other.

If everyone were exactly the same size there would be no perceptions of small and tall people. To get a grasp of what a tall person is we must have some notion what a person who is not tall is like. Furthermore, a western man who comes to McLeod Ganj may find that Tibetans who see him think of him as tall or big on the basis that he is somewhat taller and more heavily built than most Tibetans. Back in his own country however he may be no more than average-sized person, who nobody thinks of as tall. It is only in reliance upon the appearance of other phenomena, and in comparison with them, that any particular object can be designated as big or small, beautiful or ugly, good or bad and so forth. If we are asked, "Is this big?" strictly speaking we can only reply 'Big in relation to what?' Often the kind of perception we have of an object relies very much on past experience. Take momos for instance. Tibetans are very fond of these steamed dumplings especially when they are filled with meat. On the other hand, vegetarians or somebody who ate momos before and got very sick would perhaps find them most unpleasant to eat. In themselves are momos pleasant tasting, unpleasant, or neither? No general answer can be given, only an answer from a particular point of view, in reliance upon a comparison with other tastes and flavours.

Meeting, the third aspect of dependent-arising explained by the Consequentialists, stresses the way in which a multitude of different factors come together in any act of cognition. For any object to be cognized there has to be the meeting of the object with the consciousness apprehending it. More specifically it is the parts of the object assembled together which cast their aspect to the mind and produce an apprehension of the object. Any entity we grasp at as having a single identity in fact results from many different aspects of meeting or coming together to form it. As an example, take a product such as a knife. It comes about through the meeting of its causes, some iron for the blade and a piece of wood for the handle, the craftsmen involved the heat of the forge, the hammer and the cutting, grinding and polishing tolls. Then there is the coming together of its parts, the blade, the haft and rivets or glue which fasten them together. Finally the collection of parts meets with a consciousness which knows what the distinguishing characteristics of a knife are and that consciousness interprets the assemblage of parts as a knife.

Contemplating dependent-arising under the three headings of dependent-arising, relying and meeting will enrich our understanding and put at our fingertips many ways of reasoning against our ingrained grasping at inherent existence. When we recollect how thoroughly dependent our own existence is on the labour of multitude of others, will not that help to reduce our self-satisfied pride? When we consider that the people who are the object of our anger are not a worthy object of anger from their own side, but are merely grasped as such by our own rampaging mind, will not that rob our anger of the fuel that feeds it? Practically speaking, long before we are able to convince ourselves with watertight logical proof that all phenomena are utterly devoid of existence by their own power, we can use our limited understanding of dependent-arising to catch our negative emotions before they boil up and become really poisonous. Once we are in the throes of a fit of jealousy or rage our mind is generally too turbulent to steer onto a different course. But by analysing what went wrong afterwards and recollecting frequently the various facets of dependent-arising we can gradually reduce the frequency and intensity of our negative emotions.

Other benefits of remembering dependent-arising were spoken of by Buddha as three. Firstly, remembering dependent-arising will keep us from falling to either of the two extremes, the extreme of permanence or the extreme of nihilism. When we recollect that all things are interdependent, we will not grasp at ourselves and other phenomena as being inherently existent. By focusing on how all things are dependently-related we will realize that they can only be related in the first place by virtue of the fact that they exist. The first recognition will prevent us falling to the extreme of permanence and the second will prevent us from falling to the extreme of nihilism. Secondly, understanding dependent-arising will enable us to recognize correctly how phenomena exist only nominally through the conventions of terminology. The third benefit is that we will be able to understand clearly how phenomena are like a magician's illusions or reflections in water. Up until the verses quoted at the beginning of this chapter, the explanation of dependent-arising has been directed towards realizing the emptiness of inherent existence of phenomena. What the verses at the beginning of this section reveal is that understanding emptiness thoroughly leads one to a still better understanding of dependent-arising. The most profound aspects of dependent-arising, it is said, do not become clear until after one has realized emptiness.

We will come to Tsong Khapa's description of phenomena as being like illusions in a later verse, but the question of what this nominal existence is that is left after we have proved that phenomena do not exist by way of their own entities or characteristics is a pertinent one and is a point over which the Consequentialists part company with the other Buddhist schools. The other schools' position is that if one rejects inherent existence then it is tantamount to rejecting existence as such. Without inherent existence nothing would exist, or else any appearance to mind would have to be accepted as valid. The Consequentialists reply that just because what exists is merely imputed, it does not follow that whatever is imputed exists. A man who sees a rabbit in the distance with its ears sticking up might think that he is seeing a rabbit with horns. This does not mean that a horned rabbit exits. When the man thinks, 'That rabbit has got horns,' the basis of designation, an ordinary rabbit, and the object designated, a rabbit having horns, do not have the compatibility necessary for the imputation to stick, as we discussed earlier in our example of the rope and the snake. By abandoning the idea of there being a solid core, existing from the object's own side, on which the object can be designated, we can follow the Consequentialists' inspiration and experiment with the experience of all things as empty or selfless, but, unless we have a sound way to posit the things of the world such as cows, trees, chairs and rabbits we will only have succeeded in plunging to the abyss of nihilism. Two lines of thought which are exclusive to the Consequentialists can be set forth to indicate ways in which the existence of the phenomena of the world can be upheld after inherent existence has been repudiated. The first concerns the mutual reliance of parts and whole; the second concerns accepting things as merely nominally existent, dependent on terms or designates.

If we think about a sprout and ask where it came from, we can say it came from a seed. The seed in turn was produced by an earlier plant, which itself was once a seed. The beginning of this process of seeds and sprouts producing each other is lost in time. The I or self is something which is apprehended in dependence on the aggregates or parts of a person. And what does the apprehension of a part such as the body depend on? It's parts, the limbs, the torso and the head? Is the torso also only apprehended in dependence on its parts in turn, and those parts on their parts? Is the process of apprehending a person a virtually endless one when we examine it, like the process of the production of seeds and plants? This is surely rather an unwieldy way of positing the conventional person. Nevertheless, the lower schools are obliged to resort to this description of the process. They do not say the person is devoid of inherent existence of course. But, since they deny the existence of a person who is substantially existent in the sense of being self-sufficient, they have to be able to describe how a person can be imputed on to any of his or her aggregates. The Consequentialists, rather than going through this endless explanation simply say that a person is established in dependence on the aggregates of a person and the aggregates of a person are established in dependence upon a person.

For instance, suppose we are standing at the edge of a jungle and we hear the roar of an animal which we recognize to be the sound of a tiger. We can only recognize the sound as the sound of a tiger if we know what a tiger is and judge that there is one lurking in the undergrowth. At the same time, it is only the roar of the tiger that indicates to us the presence of a tiger, supposing we can neither see nor smell the beast. In this situation our realization of a tiger and the sound of tiger are simultaneous and mutually dependent. This is how those refute inherent existence affirm all the phenomena of the world, through their dependent relationships with each other. There is no fixed independent essence to any phenomena but phenomena are not thereby merely figments of our imagination like the child of a barren woman. When phenomena are imputed to their parts no endless chains of imputation of parts upon smaller parts are observed but the cognition of the whole and the parts each rely on the other. This reliance is like an old man who gets up with the aid of stick. In order to rise, the man leans on his stick. The man is therefore supported by his stick, but at the same time, the stick is supported by the man. Without the man to place the stick in the upright position and hold it, the stick would be unable to perform the function of bearing the man's weight. All phenomena participate in these relationships of mutual dependence. However, it is said that this aspect of dependent-arising only becomes completely clear after we have realized emptiness.

Understanding how to accept all things as mere designations means recognizing how they exist only nominally, through the conventions of terminology, which was classed above as the second benefit of realizing dependent-arising. As our example here we can take anger. Under the influence of anger our powers of sensible decision fly out of the window and we do many regrettable things. It is thus very beneficial to control it. Discovering the emptiness of inherent existence of anger, the person who is angry and the object of anger is a supreme antidote but trying to apply this antidote once the anger has erupted is not easy. After the anger has subsided we should analyse it and try to isolate it. Anger manifests in various ways: we clench our muscles; our hearts beat faster; our face goes red; our voice rises to a scream; perhaps we pour forth stream of invective; we have a rampant blind urge to destroy the object of our anger, but we cannot point a finger at any of these manifestations and identify any one of them as the actual anger. Within the mind itself during the time we are angry, different aspects can be mentally identified: there is the feeling of being let down or deprived of something; there is also a feeling of grievance where the blame is focused on another person or an object; there is the part of the mind which instigates the action of lashing out with hand or tongue. None of these can be pinpointed as the actual anger. Analysing thoroughly in this fashion we arrive again at the point where we cannot find anything from the side of the object which is that object. We have a group of characteristics, none of which itself is anger, which between them amount to something which performs the function of anger. Anger is merely designated to this base of designation. If we perform an ultimate analysis, looking for the anger that exists from its own side, we find nothing. This mere absence constitutes the emptiness of inherent existence of anger and should be meditated on as much as possible. The only anger that can be found is one that exists merely in terms of a designation. One has to be satisfied with this mere nominal existence of anger simply because no other mode of existence can be identified. There are certain characteristics or manifestations which act as the basis of the designation. There is the consciousness which does the designating. Then there is the designation or term applied by that consciousness to that basis, according to the conventions of terminology. If we try to find something deeper, something underneath the name that is the object, we will be unsuccessful. We can only keep coming back to the designation itself. Again this is the subtle aspect of dependent-arising which the realization of emptiness is said to assist us in cognizing. So, dependent-arising is in the first place the supreme reasoning that leads to a realization of emptiness but then a realization of emptiness in turn leads back to a more thorough-going appreciation of dependent-arising.

If we thoroughly understand that anger and the person who is angry are empty of inherent existence, we will become free of our bondage to anger. But realising that things are not inherently existent should not lead us to reject conventional reality and view all discrimination as a hindrance. As the great Indian master of logic Dharmakirti says in his Commentary on Valid Cognition:

> With the aid of sounds, terms are imputed;
> This is for conventional (understanding).
> The purpose of words ends there—
> Is this clear to you?

> The skilful accept worldly conventions
> Because in dependence on them
> They can lead people to their object of attainment,
> The ultimate goal.

Verse 11 of Tsong Khapa's text indicates how closely emptiness of inherent existence and dependent-arising are related; one is the 'meaning' of the other, and the denial of inherent existence does not negate the phenomena of the world. Verse 12 indicates that those who cannot see that emptiness and dependent-arising are dependently related are making a fatal error. Either they cling to the reality of actions and reject emptiness, or they embrace emptiness and see all activity and discrimination as meaningless. In either case they tumble from the middle way into the abyss of perplexity. Most people's instinctive tendency is to go to the first extreme of grasping things to be inherently existent. They have to refute the inherent or 'independent' existence of things, which is like a sky flower or the horn of a rabbit, utterly non-existent. When one breaks down one's habitual assumptions and one first realizes that things are devoid of independent existence, at that time there is said to be a particular tendency to veer towards the other extreme of thinking that things are 'totally non-existent.'

VII

Illussion and Reality

15. Thus it is taught that because nothing exists
     Other than the dependently-arisen
     There is no existing thing
     Which is not empty of inherent existence.

16. Since inherent existence can never come to an end
     If phenomena had any inherent nature,
     Nirvana would be impossible,
     And all fabrications could not be stopped.

Verse 15 and 16 develop the main theme of the *Praise for Dependent-Arising*; that there is no phenomena of the past, present or future that is inherently existent and not dependently existent. Being inherently existent is simply impossible. If something was inherently or intrinsically established then no causes or circumstances could have any effect on it. Once in existence it would never succumb to change and disappear or transform into something else. If the delusions in the mind of the sentient being who became the enlightened one of our era, Shakyamuni Buddha, were intrinsically established, how could he ever have got rid of them? How could 'elaborations,' meaning deluded conceptual minds, be stopped? If he inherently existed as a being in cyclic existence how could he have left it and entered the state beyond suffering? For him 'Nirvana would be impossible' (Verse 16). Not even the Buddhas, nor the dharma, nor the Sangha, none of the Three Jewels to which the Buddhist goes for refuge, exist from their own side. Emptiness itself is also empty of inherent existence. Even some scholars within the Buddhist fold have held that emptiness has some absolute status beyond the interplay of dependent-arising. Emptiness is called ultimate truth, which might lead to the impression that is an absolute, objective reality transcending the relative. But this is far from being the case. The emptiness of inherent existence, for example, of a tree is called an ultimate truth because it is a phenomena such that, when it is perceived directly, the way it appears to the mind and the ways it actually exists are completely concordant. On the other hand a tree is called a conventional truth because it is a phenomena such that when it is perceived by anyone except a Buddha, the way it appears and the way it actually exists are not concordant, since a tree always appears to the mind of anyone who is not a Buddha to be inherently existent, but it is not. So emptiness is given the name 'ultimate' because the only consciousness that experiences it directly is one that has removed all the superimpositions of ignorance.

If we meditate deeply on the emptiness of the self and the objects of use of the self for a long period of time, gradually ignorance and the other delusions will be erased from our minds forever. Meditation on emptiness is the most powerful antidote for sufferings of cyclic existence there is, but of itself emptiness cannot do anything. From its own side it has no power or intention to relieve us of our sufferings. It is just one facet of the way things are. It is not something that anyone bows down to and worships. It is not an ultimate in the way that, for instance, the Christian God might perhaps be called "the ultimate one." It may be thought of it in terms of individual phenomena. We can reflect very fruitfully on the emptiness of a cup or a table for example. Just remembering that without a cup there would be no emptiness of inherent existence of a cup establishes that the emptiness of inherent existence of a cup is a dependent-arising, since it is dependent on the cup.

17.   Therefore, who could challenge him
      Who, in assemblies of the wise,
      Has clearly proclaimed with lion's roar
      "Things do not have inherent existence."

18.   Since lack of inherent nature
      And the ability to function do not contradict,
      Never mind that dependent-arising
      And emptiness co-exist.

19. 'By the reason of dependent-arising,
     There are no grounds for extreme views.'
     For this fine teaching, O Protector,
     Your speech is unexcelled.

20. 'All is empty of self-nature!'
     And, 'From this cause arises that effect!'
     These two knowledges assist each other
     And abide in harmony.

21. What is more wonderful than this?
     What is more marvellous than this?
     If you are praised for this principle,
     That is real praise, nothing else.

At the time the Buddha taught in India, many different schools of philosophy and many different esoteric mental disciplines which were supposed to be the key to liberation existed. Before these scholars and adepts listened to Buddha's teachings, none of them had heard about dependent-arising and emptiness, but once his teachings were revealed to them they had nothing with which to rebut his formidable arguments in the 'assemblies of the wise' (verse 17). Some of Buddha's first disciples were famous teachers in their own right. Shariputra and Maudgalyayana were two whose followers are said to have numbered in the hundreds. When they heard Buddha's teachings proclaimed: 'By the reason of dependent-arising there are no grounds for extreme views' (verse 19) and 'All is empty of self-nature!' (verse 20), they found nothing to equal them in either profundity or extensiveness. When these noted teachers converted to Buddhism they brought their many followers with them, the twin ideas of dependent-arising and emptiness being the unique teachings of Buddha's system that won them over. Buddha's teaching that these two, dependent-arising and emptiness assist or mutually support each other is the principle of verse 21 that Buddha is worthy to be praised for above all else.

22. Those held in slavery by delusions,
     Hopelessly resent you (so free and clear).
     Small wonder that they find intolerable
     That sound of, 'Non-inherent existence.'

23.   But to accept dependent-arising,
       The precious treasure of your speech,
       Then resent the roar of emptiness;
       This do I find surprising.

24.   If through the very term of highest
       Dependent-arising, the door that leads
       To non-inherent existence, they grasp
       Inherent existence, by what means

25.   Can these people be led into
       That good path which pleases you,
       That incomparable entrance,
       Well travelled by supreme Aryas?

There were also those who remained unattracted to Buddha's teachings. They are mentioned in verse 22 as being "held in slavery by delusions."

The followers of the one nihilistic, non-Buddhist, school were called Charvakas (Hedonists). Because they denied any validity to reasoning and denied past and future lives they were judged to have fallen to the extreme of nihilism. After the Buddhist view became well-known, other Hindu schools in India decided that there were now two schools that had veered to the extreme of nihilism, the Charvakas and the Buddhists! Even today there are scholars within the Indian tradition and also in the west who conclude that the Buddhists of the Consequentialist persuasion advance a completely nihilistic view. "Small wonder that they find intolerable/That sound of, 'non-inherent existence.'" It is not so surprising if those who do not have much understanding of dependent-arising reject what dependent-arising is supposed to prove, non-inherent existence, but that people who have studied dependent-arising and declare that they accept it should also spurn its natural consequence, emptiness—this Tsong Khapa does find contrary to expectations (verse 23). As we have seen, the stance of these thinkers, followers of the lower Buddhist schools, is to adhere to a rather more limited vision of dependent-arising. Buddha taught explicitly about emptiness in the *Perfection of Wisdom Sutras*. The response of some of the followers of the two lowest schools, the Particularists and the Sutra followers, is to deny that these discourses were actually taught by the Buddha; and to say that the great clarifier of these teachings, Nagarjuna, does not deserve to be called a holder of the Buddhist view. Others from these two lower schools say that these discourses were only taught for small numbers of disciples and are not to be taken literally. The Mind Only followers and Autonomists accept the *Perfection of Wisdom Sutras* as the Buddha's word, but also call them interpretive, rather than definitive scriptures, meaning that they should not be taken at face value; rather, the intended meaning is different from the apparent one.

Having arrived at the very gate of understanding non-inherent existence by having some understanding of dependent-arising then, these people fail to pass through the gate and follow the path which pleases the Buddhas. Those who follow this path are 'Aryas' (verse 25), or Superior beings, that is, people who have realized emptiness directly and are in the process of applying the actual antidote to deluded ignorance by familiarising themselves single-pointedly with emptiness again and gain.

26.   Inherent existence, unmade and non-dependent;
        Dependently-related, made and dependent;
        How can these two states be combined
        On one base, without contradiction?

27.   Therefore, whatever arises dependently
        Though always free of inherent existence,
        Appears to exist from its own side;
        So you said this is like an illusion.

In this verse Buddha compares all phenomena to an illusion. Notice that he does not say all phenomena are illusions, merely that they are like illusions. The kind of illusion referred to by the Buddha is an illusion conjured up by an Indian magician of the type who is able to cause a pebble or a stick to appear as a horse or an elephant or as a beautiful woman to his audience by casting a mantra that affects their eyes. The illusion appears to be a real horse, an elephant or woman but, in truth, is not. Possibly this type of magician is not so common now as in the days of ancient India, although the modern-day hypnotist is able to foster similar illusions in the minds of his subjects. But for a modern equivalent that will be within the direct experience of everyone we can use the example of images seen in films or on television. When children who are too young to understand the nature of the pictures that appear on television see what appears to be people, animals or food on a television screen they think these things are actually in space before them or inside the television. The way we apprehend these images is different. We readily associate them with the objects they represent but we do not grasp at them as being the actual objects. Sometimes when we watch television a very small image appears in the center of the screen, the image, say, of a car or a box of soap powder. The image grows bigger and bigger. This represents the object coming towards us. A young child or naive person who has never watched television before thinks that there is an object actually coming nearer to him. If we were asked if there was an object actually coming towards us, we would reply that of course there was not. Note, however, that although we are too sophisticated to take this illusion as real, even we can become so far immersed in the flickering images that we are filled now with fear, now with desire, mirth or sorrow.

The way ordinary people see phenomena is very similar to the way the young child sees the things that appear on television and to the way the magician's subjects see his illusory horse. The common factor is that in all three cases the viewer unconsciously superimposes onto the object viewed a mode of existence which the object does not possess. The image of a dog the child sees on television appears to be a real dog. The illusory horse is taken to be a real horse by those under the magician's spell. Objects, which are not inherently existent, appear to us to be inherently existent and we grasp at or assent to that appearance. When we who have both a strong appearance of inherent existence and a strong grasping at it hear for the first time that there is no such thing as inherent existence it may strike us as incredible. It runs very much counter to the view of the world that is ingrained in us and this appearance of inherent existence is no easy thing to dislodge. The water of a mirage on a road on a hot day persists in appearing as real water even when we know well that it is only an optical illusion caused by atmospheric conditions. Similarly even when Aryas or Superior beings, who are able to meditate on the emptiness of inherent existence single-pointedly and directly, arise from meditation they still have the appearance of phenomena as inherently existent. But one great difference between those Superior beings and ordinary people is that the former do not assent to this deceptive appearance of inherent existence.

When an ordinary person sees an object such as a pair of shoes or a television in a shop window, the object in the first place appears to that being's eye conscious-ness as inherently existent. Then in the case where the person becomes attracted to the object, his discrimination that the object is desirable and his subsequent wish to possess it are induced and strengthened up by the mind which grasps at the object to exist from its own side. In this frame of mind, the person grasps that the object's ability to give the owner of it happiness is intrinsic to the object. The object's gleaming, brand-new appearance makes it particularly appealing. If we think about it, even this aspect is grasped at as inherent in the object, and not discounted as something that will have vanished in the first week of use. Beyond that there is a third level of being affected by the superimposed factor of inherent existence. This occurs when the person actually takes possession of the object. At this time the attachment induced by grasping the object to be inherently existent and inherently pleasant mixes with attachment which arises from thinking, 'This object is mine,' while grasping the self to be inherently existent. We can also describe how the feeling of hatred towards, say, someone whom we discriminate as an enemy, first arises and then intensifies to an altogether exaggerated degree in three stages: firstly the stage of the mere appearance of inherent existence; secondly, the stage of assenting to and grasping at that appearance and thereupon generating hatred; and thirdly the stage of very strong hatred when grasping at our own self as inherently existent comes into the equation as well. In the train of these strong delusions come deluded actions. Through attachment we indulge in acts of miserliness or violence to clutch on to our possessions. Out of hatred we descend to abuse, slander, scorn and far, far worse.

Superior beings (as we said, those who have seen emptiness directly), with the exception of Buddhas, still have the first of the above three stages, in which phenomena appear to them as inherently existent, but they are not deceived by this appearance. They know that it is in truth an illusion, so they are at the point where they can abandon engaging in actions which perpetuate the cycle of death and rebirth. They do not develop delusions in dependence upon the appearance of inherent existence, and not generating these delusions they do not engage in negative actions. For this reason they do not create new causes to be reborn in cyclic existence. There is a further development when a Superior of the Great Vehicle lineage attains Buddhahood. Not only does a Buddha Superior not grasp at things as inherently existent, but, it is said, at that time things cease even to appear as inherently existent to him. What does a being who has reached the state of the highest enlightenment see then? It is said that the Buddha does not see conventional truths, that is, the phenomena of the world, such as house, clouds and trees from his own point of view. Rather, he understands the appearance of these conventional phenomena from the point of view of ordinary beings. He is said to apprehend conventional phenomena simply by knowing what ordinary beings are experiencing. This is an explanation which may well sound inconceivable when we first hear it. Our ordinary understanding finds it difficult to expand far enough to encompass a Buddha's surpassing qualities of realization and compassionate action. Only a Buddha is said to be able to fully comprehend the good qualities of a Buddha. Nevertheless, explanations of how phenomena are like an illusion, in appearing to exists inherently while not so existing, are within the scope of reasoning, and, in spite of some people's initial reaction to these teachings as far-fetched and fanciful, if we think about them carefully we will come to see that in the end the only way any phenomena can possibly exist is as a dependent-arising, devoid of intrinsic identity.

28.   Through this very fact we can well understand
       The assertion that, in the way you taught,
       Those who would challenge you
       By way of logic can find no fallacy.

29.   Why? Because your explanation
       Makes remote the chance that one
       Will exaggerate or deny
       Manifest or non-manifest things.

30. Your speech is seen as peerless
Because it presents the path of dependent-arising,
And this gives rise to certainty
That (your) other teachings are valid too.

Thus, as it implies in verse 28, the one who can overturn the Buddha's teachings on the way things exist has not yet been born. On the philosophical side of the teachings Buddhism takes its stand squarely on logic and reasoning. That is why the Buddha's teachings offer such a clear path of mental development. In verse 29 'manifest' and 'non-manifest' things refers to phenomena that we can experience directly with our senses and to phenomena that we can only initially comprehend by using reasoning, respectively. These two categories cover all phenomena. Exaggerating phenomena means ascribing to them a mode of existence that they do not have. Denying them means not recognizing a mode of existence that they do in fact possess. We can investigate for ourselves whether the teachings on emptiness and dependent-arising are true or not using our reasoning powers. Other aspects of the Buddha's teachings are less amenable to reasoning, for instance his teaching that generosity in this life leads one to enjoy resources in future lives and the practice of ethical behaviour in this life leads one to enjoy happiness in future lives. In verse 30 Tsong Khapa indicates that directly realizing emptiness as he did will inspire such a respect for the insight of the teacher who taught it that one will have great confidence that those other less easily verifiable aspects of the Buddha's teachings are true too.

31. You saw reality, and taught it well.
Those who train in your footsteps
Will transcend all troubles,
For they shall destroy the root of evil.

32. But those who turn away from your teaching,
Though they wearily struggle, long and hard,
Are like inviting more problems
As the view of self is further strengthened.

33. Marvellous! When the wise comprehend
The difference between these two (trainings),

> How can they fail to respect you
> From their innermost hearts?

The next set of verses, 31 to 33, compares the prospects of those who follow in the footsteps of the Buddha and those who look elsewhere for direction. Seeing what the Buddha saw about the way things exist does not simply bring about the abstract satisfaction of finding out something that happens to be true, but it means that one has at last arrived at a view which is contradictory to and can displace the deep-rooted grasping at a self of persons and phenomena, the deceptive perspective which leads us again and again into harming others and bringing all suffering on to ourselves. Without identifying this deeply embedded misunderstanding about the self as the fundamental source of all our troubles any other attempts to find happiness will only be treating the symptoms of the disease rather than the source of it. As we have already suggested to try to describe what the Buddha saw when he 'saw reality' (verse 31) is extremely difficult. One more clue we can take account of is that Buddha and only a Buddha can see a phenomena's conventional and ultimate nature simultaneously. This signifies for instance that he sees both a cup and the emptiness of inherent existence of that cup together at the same time. People who have realized emptiness directly but who have not reached Buddha-hood can observe either the conventional nature or the ultimate one, not both simultaneously.

When we try to conceive of the experience of realizing just the ultimate nature of an object such as a cup or the self, it may be helpful in terms of an analogy to think about empty space. This phenomena has some similarities with emptiness in the way it appears to the mind. Both these phenomena are permanent, which means they are static and not changing from moment to moment in a causal series. Both are understood only in terms of there being an absence of some other phenomena. The meaning of space or uncaused space is lack of obstruction and contact. Due to there being an underlying absence of obstruction and contact, forms that occupy space such as houses, our bodies and cups have room to exist in the place they do. Due to there being empty space in a cup, it can be filled with something such as tea. But this lack of obstruction and contact does not have any implied qualities. The absence of a coin in our hand is similar. Such a phenomena is only cognized by bringing our idea of a coin to mind, looking for one in the hand and then negating it. In the same way we can only understand emptiness by first of all bringing our idea of inherent existence to mind, searching for it and then negating it. Although we grasp at objects to be inherently existent all the time, it requires plenty of thought about dependent-arising before we can single out the superimposed aspect of inherent existence. This we must do with exact precision before we can negate it and meditate on its absence. So, as when cognizing empty space, one is essentially cognizing a lack of something when one perceives emptiness. In the latter case it is the absence of something whose existence one formerly took for granted. To say that an experience of emptiness is like having a vision of light or something like that could be misleading therefore, in that light, being form, has positive qualities, whereas emptiness is only a state of negation. One person in Tibet went around proclaiming that he had realized emptiness. He was asked to describe it and he said it was like a pigeon. After that he was given the nickname, Professor Pigeon! But, from what other people say, we can suggest that when one experiences emptiness one experiences a very relaxed sort of feeling. Due to our delusions, our mind is in a state of constant agitation, like boiling water. Disturbing states of mind are constantly arising; conceptions and projections bubble up endlessly. When one realizes emptiness it is as though someone pours a large amount of cold water onto that boiling water, which then becomes cool and very still. The mind becomes relaxed and clear in a way it never has been before. We should not be discouraged by thinking that emptiness is very difficult to realize correctly. We should do all we can to understand it even on a very gross level because this will plant imprints on our minds to realize it more precisely in the future. Finally, in order to realize emptiness and see reality we cannot neglect the other aspects of the path, such as training in ethical conduct, loving kindness, concentration and so on. These help to purify, energize and inspire the mind to focus powerfully on the subtleties of the correct view.

34.   Not to mention the entire wealth of your teachings,
       Just a rough understanding of
       One small part of them,
       Is to bring supreme bliss.

35.   Alas! My own mind was ruled by confusion
      Even though I took refuge long ago
      To such heap of qualities
      I do not possess even a part of the quality.

36.   Yet before the stream of life has sunk
      Into the mouth of the Lord of Death,
      I have developed a little belief in you.
      Even this I think is fortunate.

However, if we did only have a chance to understand 'one small part' of the teachings, the part that would bring supreme bliss above all is the teachings on dependent-arising. This is how we can interpret verse 34. Verses 35 and 36 strike a more personal note. Tsong Khapa relates how little he understood of the Buddha's teachings when first he went for refuge. But now, having finally gained a deep understanding of the essence of the Buddha's wisdom, he is able to see exactly why Buddha is the ultimate refuge. Even though Tsong Khapa is revered as one of the very greatest scholars and adepts who reinvigorated and clarified the Buddhist doctrine in Tibet and left behind a magnificent corpus of writings including commentaries of the most penetrating kind, it seems that when he is compared to the Buddha himself, the Buddha's qualities are vaster still. If we stand by the side of an extensive lake the expanse of water may seem enormous, but in comparison to it the waters of an ocean are far wider and still deeper.

VIII

Conclusion

37. Of teachers, the teachers of dependent-arising.
    Of wisdom, the wisdom of dependent-arising;
    These two are like kings conquering the world,
    Only you and no one else know this well and perfectly.

The Buddha's unique qualities that made his appearance in this world-system inestimably valuable were his possessing the wisdom of dependent-arising and his teaching of it. Otherwise ones who preceded the Buddha or appeared subsequently, even if they had any understanding of dependent-arising they failed to teach it to a wide audience, or if on the other hand, they were eloquent and skilful teachers, they lacked wisdom and had nothing to say about dependent-arising. Having the teachings on dependent-arising still available together with the wisdom realizing those teachings is said to be like still enjoying the Buddha's presence in our world today.

38. All that you have taught
    Is related to dependent-arising;
    And that also for transcending suffering.
    You perform no deeds that wouldn't bring peace.

39. Wonderful is your teaching!
    Since whoever listens
    Will attain peace, who could not
    Be devoted to preserving such teachings?

40. As it overcomes all opponents,
    Is free from internal contradictions
    And fulfils both goals of beings,
    My delight ever grows for this Doctrine.

Even though the teachings of the Buddha are very extensive, in terms of the range of subjects covered and thoroughness with which they are explained all of them relate directly or indirectly to the profound dependent-arising, since this is the very essence of them. As we have reviewed a few of the differences between the four different tenet systems that have been codified from the great collection of teachings, we have noted teachings that are quite contradictory to one another. In one place Buddha allowed that the self inherently exists. In another he refuted inherent existence with abundant reasons. This is but a variety of approaches to the one goal of leading beings of all different aptitudes to an unmistaken understanding of the full meaning of dependent-arising at its deepest level. For instance, there was a king called Ajata-shatru who ruled over a certain part of India at the time of the Buddha. He was so evil that he had even murdered his own father and mother in order to gain the throne for himself. His way of life was therefore utterly contrary to the one that Buddha was teaching. He developed a strong antipathy towards the Buddha and tried to kill him too, once by sending a mad elephant charging towards where the Buddha was teaching in the hope that he might be trampled to death. This king rejected the idea that there were any higher beings who could be an object of refuge for people. He rejected the necessity for practising virtue and also the existence of past and future lives. However, his mother and father had great faith in the Buddha and they both had led virtuous lives. The father had spoken to his son many times about the Buddha's teachings. When he was killed he was reborn in a celestial realm. He then showed himself in the form a deity to his son. His son received a great shock when this happened and his former materialistic outlook was completely overturned. He saw that there were past and future lives and became very afraid of the future consequences of having killed his mother and father. The king decided to go to the Buddha and throw himself at his feet. The Buddha was aware of this and knew that if he told the king, once he had made his confession, how intensely negative the act of killing one's parents is, then the king would be plunged into such great despair that he might even die from it. The Buddha therefore understood that on this occasion telling the bald truth would not be beneficial. So what the Buddha said to the king was that in order to practise dharma the first thing one should do is to kill one's mother and father. Then one should kill the king of the kingdom, then his two chief ministers, all his attendants, than all the servants of the attendants. The king was extremely fascinated by this teaching and was amazed that the Buddha should have taught it. With his overwhelming anxiety about his actions diverted in this way, the king was able to think more clearly, and, back in his palace, he pondered what the Buddha had said. He understood the Buddha to be a person who had abandoned violence in all its form, yet here he was teaching that one should kill people in order to find liberation from suffering. The king pondered further and eventually reached the understanding that the superficial level of the teaching was a device to trap his attention, while on another level killing one's father and mother referred to destroying the root ignorance and the karma which springs from that ignorance. Ignorance and karma lead to rebirth in cyclic existence. In this way they are like the father and mother from whom all beings in cyclic existence are born. Killing the king of the kingdom refers to eliminating the states of mind which instigate actions that cause rebirth in cyclic existence. The mind is the instigator of all unskilful actions and within the context of a person, the mind is like the king in a kingdom. These three elements, ignorance, karma and conscious-ness are the first three of the twelve links of dependent-arising. The two chief ministers that have to be killed can either be interpreted as two more of the twelve links or as the two extremes, the views of permanence and nihilism. The rest of the twelve links are what is referred to by the royal attendants. Then the servants of the attendants refers to all the objects in cyclic existence. So the Buddha's implicit teaching was that if one eliminates all these, one will attain liberation, by bringing the production of the twelve links of dependent-arising to a halt. By the time King Ajata-shatru had deduced all this, a great faith in the Buddha had awakened in him and he went on to become one of the major patrons of the Buddha in those days. This is one example of the way in which Buddha had a special ability to guide beings with different dispositions along different paths to a full understanding of dependent-arising. It also shows how 'internal con-tradictions' (verse 40) between different teachings that are apparent on the superficial level are resolved when their full import becomes clear.

Also in verse 40, the two 'goals of beings' that the Buddha's teachings fulfils are the goals of oneself and of others. The Buddha is not just someone who has achieved peace for himself but has also perfected his capacity to bring others to peace. He does not just teach the path to individual liberation but also the more arduous stages of evolving to the higher state of complete enlightenment for the benefit of all. Just how difficult and long this second path can be is indicated in verse 41.

41.   For the sake of this Doctrine you gave
       Again and again over countless aeons,
       Sometimes your body, sometimes your life,
       Your dear family, and treasures of wealth.

The path to full enlightenment is called the way of a bodhisattva. A bodhisattva is someone who is dedicated to achieving Buddhahood for all beings. His understanding of emptiness has to be more extensive than that of someone going to individual liberation and also the bodhisattva must accumulate a far vaster store of virtues, serving the welfare of others over and over again for countless lifetimes.

In the last section of *Praise for Dependent-Arising* before the concluding verses Tsong Khapa reveals some of his personal experiences in trying to follow this very path of the bodhisattva warrior. No individual dramatic acts of self-sacrifice are recorded, but the picture of a life of unswerving dedication is conveyed by the string of illuminating images. They describe the uplift of energy and the protection from sorrow which flow from pure faith in one's teacher and the blissful relief of finally coming to the actual quintessential meaning of the teachings, the experience which inspired these words. And if anyone should ask about Tsong Khapa's efforts on behalf of other sentient beings, we have only to point to his teachings, such as this *Praise* itself, as evidence of his lifelong devotion to helping others by transmitting to them the Buddha's speech and thus inspiring them to abandon sorrow.

42.   By seeing your qualities
       As a fish is drawn by the hook;
       How sad my fate to have not heard from you
       This teaching that you got so attracted.

43. The intensity of this sadness
    Does not let my mind go free,
    Just as a mother's mind never separates
    From the thought of her beloved, lost child.

44. But when I reflect on your speech, thinking,
    'Blazing with splendour of holy marks and signs,
    Haloed by rays of light,
    O Teacher, with your beautiful Brahma voice,

45. You spoke in this way,' then in my mind
    The image of Shakyamuni arises and
    Immediately my sorrows are healed,
    As moonbeams sooth a fever.

The first of the series of images describes how he is captivated by the good qualities of the dharma like a fish hooked tight, but feels a piercing sadness at not having heard the teachings from the Buddha himself. Through great faith, the Buddha appears instead to his mind's eye, splendidly arrayed, discoursing in a melodious voice. A circle of disciples was fortunate enough to be present when the Buddha turned the wheel of dharma in person. Visualizing himself as one of those, he receives blessings which dissolve his sorrows. Tsong Khapa compares these blessings to moonbeams which are able to soothe the torment of heat. In a country like India the days can be oppressively hot, but when the moon comes out in the evening, its rays seem to have a pacifying, cooling effect. People are sensitive to moonlight in different ways however. A few people find the moon's influence disturbing. It makes them restless and unable to sleep, even very lively.

46. Even with this marvellous and good system,
    The unskilled become totally confused,
    Just like an individual
    Who does not know how to untangle a *balbaza* grass

47. Seeing this I made every effort
    To follow the learned scholars,
    And repeatedly sought
    The meaning of your intention.

48.   I studied many treatises
      Of Buddhist and non-Buddhist schools,
      My mind was then tormented sorely,
      Time and again in the web of doubt.

49.   Nagarjuna was prophesied to explain rightly
      The principle of your final vehicle,
      Free from the extremes of existence and non-existence.
      His treatises are like a night lily garden.

50.   One Whose bright orb of immaculate wisdom is fully developed
      Moving freely across the sky of scripture,
      Dispelling the darkness of extremist hearts
      And outshining the constellations of wrong speech.

51.   Through the kindness of lama, When I see
      The illumination (of Nagarjuna's texts) by garlands of
         white light,
      The elegant explanations of glorious Chandrakirti
      My mind found relief and rest.

From the faith indicated in verses 42 to 45 arose Tsong Khapa's unquenchable enthusiasm for study. Some details of how he studied occupy the next group of verses (46 to 51). In the history of Buddhism many great beings have taken birth and have extracted from the Buddha's teachings various philosophical systems suitable to the people present at a particular time and place. Some notable names are Asanga, Nagarjuna, Bhavaviveka and Buddhapalita who were the great pioneers of the Mind-Only view, the Middle Way view, the view of the Autonomist branch of the Middle Way School and the view of the Consequentialist branch of that school respectively. The followers of these teachers were then led into many different debates on the finer points of the teachings. However, a newcomer to the Buddha's philosophy could not be expected to develop much curiosity about these disputes straight away without seeing the reason for them. He perhaps would see all the different ideas tangled together, like *balbaza* grass (verse 46), a sort of grass that grows in India, a similar plant being found in Tibet as well. It grows in huge, densely intertwined clumps and can cause irritation to the skin. On the other hand, when one develops a lot of doubts and has a desire to ask a lot of questions about the Buddhist view, then this is regarded as a favourable sign. It indicates that one has sufficient curiosity and application to make one's own attempt on these lofty peaks of wisdom. The highest, Consequentialist, view has been clearly set forth but it is said that only those of sharp intelligence can understand Buddha's ultimate intent by studying his ultimate view alone, and passively to acquiesce in the highest view, merely because our teacher says it is the highest view is not something even those who incline to 'Buddhism of the heart' rather than 'Buddhism of the head' should really be content with. It is as if Buddha deliberately delivered teachings open to different levels of interpretation in order to provoke his followers into debating one side of a question against another. In doing so we will refine and sharpen our minds to the level where we can begin to understand the truth's vital subtleties and further more we will then arrive at the correct conclusions actively, through our own power of reasoning. Thus the truth will not remain as a dogma to which we feebly assent, but will become a powerful force vanquishing confusion, bestowing clarity, and making more efficacious for doing what is good.

Tsong Khapa certainly studied the writings of the lower Buddhist schools, only to be left dissatisfied and unconvinced by their presentations (verse 48). Nonetheless his study of the lower Buddhist schools and his identification of their defects would be an entirely suitable preparation for his deeper sounding of the Consequentialist view. In one of the most beautiful metaphors of the 'Praise' (verse 49-51) , he describes how he studied the Consequentialist view mainly through the texts of Nagarjuna and Chandrakirti. Tsong Khapa wrote the *Praise for Dependent-Arising* out of his own thorough realization of the final view, and his guides for the last part of the journey to that goal were these two geniuses. Nagarjuna blazed the trail to be followed by those upholding the view that emptiness and dependent-arising are non-contradictory. Chandrakirti drew forth the meaning of Nagarjuna's texts and explained the distinctive features of the Consequentialist view very clearly. Nagarjuna's treatises are likened to a night-lily garden (verse 49). Night-lilies are so called because they are said to bloom only at night, by the light of the moon. Thus Chandrakirti, the first part of whose name means moon, is likened to the moon which bathes the garden in white light and causes the flowers of the night-lilies to open and reveal their beauties. Earlier Tsong Khapa compared the blessings that come from visualizing the Buddha to the soothing radiance of the moon. Here (verse 51) he describes how he find final relief by opening his heart to the moonbeams of pure wisdom which dispels completely the darkness of misunderstanding. Immediately he mentions the kindness of his guru, or personal teacher in guiding him to such a state of freedom.

Nagarjuna composed six texts explaining emptiness and setting out the Middle Way view. The emphasis in them is strongly on refuting the view grasping at inherent existence which was prevalent amongst the students of Buddhism of his day. Nagarjuna was both a renowned scholar and a practitioner and his texts were much studied. Opponents who were unable to discriminate between no existence and no inherent existence were quick to accuse him of denying the existence of phenomena altogether. Chandrakirti replied to these critics by setting forth not just the way in which phenomena are devoid of inherent existence but also the way in which they do nonetheless conventionally exist. Having exposed the error of acquiescing in the illusory appearance of inherent existence he proceeds to dwell on the dependently related mode of existence that phenomena do actually have. Those who are interested in finding out more about the Middle Way view should study his text, *Supplement to the Middle Way*. This would be the best introduction to Nagarjuna's works.

At the time of Tsong Khapa also there was considerable disagreement about how the view of the Middle Way should be exactly understood. Tsong Khapa received a vision of Manjushri, the deity who is the embodiment of all the Buddha's wisdom, symbolized by the flaming sword he holds aloft. In answer to Tsong Khapa's request for guidance, Manjushri directed him to rely on Chandrakirit's *Supplement to the Middle Way* as a faultless exposition by one who had complete understanding. After he had completed his own purpose by dispelling the perplexity of wrong views in his own mind, Tsong Khapa in turn composed many works which have kept the ancient flame of Buddha's profoundest wisdom burning purely for the generations who have come after him. Tsong Khapa's life was short compared to Buddha's and Nagarjuna's but he left a treasure house of commentaries and expositions of the scriptures behind. Like the Buddha we should not praise him for his realizations alone, but also for the eloquence and skill with which he offered his surpassing knowledge to others.

52.   Of all his deeds, Buddha's speech is supreme,
        And, for this very reason, true sages
        Should commemorate the Perfect One
        For this (teaching on dependent-arising).

In verse 52, Tsong Khapa singles out Buddha's 'speech,' i.e., his teaching, as his supreme deed, because this is the action which has benefitted sentient beings the most. Buddha is credited with having performed many miracles. For instance the adepts of some other Indian paths of knowledge disputed with Buddha some time after his enlightenment and engaged him in a contest of magical powers. Buddha won the contest, but where are those magical emanations and those other yogis now? When we see paintings of the miracles Buddha performed we may wonder whether these things really happened or not. In any case these fabulous deeds are lost in the past, while his teachings on the other hand are still very much with us, preserved in a pure form of words and in the minds of those with realizations.

53.   Inspired by the Teacher, I renounced the world
        And studied well the Conqueror's teaching.
        I have been diligent in yoga practice—such is
        This Bhikshu's reverence for the Great Seer.

54.   By the kindness of my guru I was fortunate to meet
        The liberating teaching of the peerless guide,
        Therefore I dedicate this virtue as a cause
        For all beings to be received by spiritual friends.

55.   Until samsara ends, may the beneficent one's teaching
        Be undisturbed by the winds of wrong views;
        May all beings in the world forever understand
        The essence of the teachings, and have faith in the teacher.

56.   May they uphold Shakyamuni's excellent way,
        Which reveals the principle of dependent-arising.
        Through all their lives let them never waver,
        Even at the cost of their bodies, or their lives.

57.   Day and night may they always be thinking
How to best propagate this glorious success
Achieved by the Supreme Liberator, in lives
Of assiduous effort beyond measure.

58.   When beings strive with pure intention (to preserve this
Doctrine)
May Brahma, Indra and the world protectors,
And the guardians, such as Mahakala,
Be constant aides, never letting them down.

These remaining six verses bring the *Praise for Dependent-Arising* to its conclusion with a prayer for auspiciousness. In verse 53 and 54 Tsong Khapa still has a little more to say about his own personal journey on the Buddhist path, of his renunciation of the world, which led him to become a monk, and of his 'yoga practice.' We should understand that not only did Tsong Khapa engage with an extraordinary degree of effort in the study of philosophy but he also did not neglect the esoteric side of Buddha's teachings. As with most of the great masters in the Tibetan tradition of Buddhism it would be a mistake to think of Tsong Khapa as only a philosopher, however distinguished; he was thoroughly versed in all aspects of Buddhist practice.

In verse 53 he pays reverence to the Buddha under the title of the Great Seer (Maharishi). This epithet of the Buddha goes back to the days before he became enlightened, to the time when he spent six years seeking that state through the practice of physical austerity. It was a path he eventually rejected but not before impressing his fellow ascetics so much with his practices of fasting, long periods of sitting upright in meditation and other forms of self-denial that they gave him the title of Great Seer. The literal meaning of the word *Rishi* (rendered *drang srong* in Tibetan) includes the senses 'honest' or 'upright' and 'to straighten.' It applies to holy men who give up worldly life, live by begging and follow a spiritual path based on physical hardship and abstinence. In the next verse Tsong Khapa again reminds the reader who might be inspired to become interested in Buddhism for the first time of the supreme importance of a personal teacher or spiritual guide. It cannot all be learned from books! Indebted as he is to the kindness of his own lama, he prays that any virtue that has been created through composing this praise may act as a cause for all beings to come under the indispensable care of such a personal teacher. Next he prays that the virtue may go in some way to protect all beings from wrong views and bestow correct understanding (verse 55). He prays that they may uphold the key principle of dependent-arising in any adversity and cause it to flourish throughout the worlds (verses 56 and 57). Finally he calls upon the worldly gods such as Brahma and Indra, upon the world protectors and the sworn protector deities of Buddhism such as Mahakala, requesting that they also do their share to spread the teachings of the Enlightened One.

If we are to derive benefit from the Buddha's teachings, in fulfilment of the spirit in which they were given, then we have to develop an interest in examining our own mind, for beyond all the other more superficial causes of enjoyment and suffering, our mind is the ultimate deciding factor in whether we are happy or not. One pre-eminent feature of the mind is that it can be trained. It tends to respond to the objects it meets in the ways it is familiar with, but can be accustomed, not always quickly, to more constructive and beneficial responses. If we find that our impulsive desires keep leading us into conflict with others and to dissatisfaction with ourselves, it is time to start examining more thoroughly where we expect those desires to lead us. We should look ahead to what the results are likely to be if those desires are indulged. If it looks in the long terms as though there is likely to be more benefit than harm caused, all well and good. What is often the case however is that we grasp at the short-term results of our actions, scarcely stopping to consider the long-term cost, either to ourselves or others. If we can create within ourselves a degree of mental freedom such that we do not become totally involved in our desires without thinking through the consequences first, then we will be making progress. Or take an unpleasant state of mind like being strongly jealous of someone. Practising the dharma can certainly eliminate such negative moods. Studying the dharma should in the first place lead us to see that it is an irrational state of mind that benefits nobody and that there are far more wholesome objects of our attention than the object of our resentment. But of course our approach has to be a balanced one. While trying to change ourselves for the better we have to accept who we are at any particular stage, without developing aversion towards our own thoughts because we cannot get rid of strong negative states of mind immediately.

When our jealousy is aroused there is not much we can do other than try to avoid being in the presence of the person who is acting as the magnet for these feelings. We have to try in whichever way we can to avoid that person. When the jealousy dies down, as it surely will, we can examine it more easily. Many of the explanations of dependent-arising and emptiness we have offered through the course of this book are very much applicable in reducing such a negative emotion. Gradually, through thinking about and discussing them we will understand how to apply them. Or, in the case of being jealous of someone because of their greater cleverness and better educational qualifications, for instance we can think 'If I become jealous of this person because they are cleverer than me, how will it benefit me? Being jealous does not lead me to have those qualities I desire. As for the effect on the other person, it neither helps nor harms him. All I am doing is bringing unhappiness on myself without any advantage at all.' Basically, in a case like this, we should aim not just to act on reasons that occur to us on the spur of the moment and fall into an all too familiar ugly mood or an unsuitable pattern of behaviour. We have to try to be objective in our examination of our motives and then we should think of as many of the negative effects of such a mood or behaviour as we can. If we are thorough about making the above investigation but still we feel we cannot trust our own judgement then perhaps we need to rely on the more objective judgement of others who are more highly developed than ourselves in their understanding of the mind. All this time, if we study the Buddha's teachings in general and try to put them into practice, then our own understanding will gradually become clearer and our ability to examine our own minds more sure.

The most important thing of all to understand is dependent-arising. In the short or medium-term Buddha's teachings can bring peace of mind in terms of being able to deal with the problems we encounter in going about everyday lives, but we should keep the long-term goal of completely realizing dependent-arising in mind. We should try to approach the understanding of it in two ways, firstly by accumulating a store of meritorious energy and ridding ourselves of previously accumulated negative energy and secondly by studying and meditating on dependent-arising, becoming more and more familiar with the ways of analysing we have explained.

Accumulating merit and eliminating negativities comes under the heading of the practice of ethics which is the first of three higher trainings mentioned earlier. A monk or nun has vows to keep. There are also vows that can be taken by lay people. Otherwise one should use the list of ten non-virtuous and ten virtuous actions to guide one's behaviour. The ten non-virtuous actions to be avoided are killing, stealing, sexual misconduct, lying, slander, harsh words, idle gossip, covetousness, wishing to harm and wrong views. The ten virtuous actions consist in definitely and deliberately not doing any of the ten non-virtues. This ethical training, over time, makes a stable and firm base of the mind and gives a chance of success to our efforts in the other two trainings of concentration and wisdom. One has to practice both of these trainings, though traditionally it is said that if one has less time one should practice the training of concentration more, whereas if one has more time to study in depth, then the training in wisdom is what one should emphasize.

Training in concentration involves developing the mind to the point where it can stay focused single-pointedly on any chosen object without wavering or becoming tired. This state is called calm-abiding. We choose a single object of meditation, such as the image of a particular Buddha, and practise placing the mind on that object again and again, only for short sessions in the beginning, but for longer and longer as time goes on. Between sessions of this type of meditation we should consider the disadvantages of cyclic existence, what causes it and how to escape from it. At other times we should think about the nature of the I and the ways in which it does and does not exist. If we mix our meditations together like this, we will ensure that our practice has a certain breadth and scope. Those of us who have more time to dwell on the training of wisdom take more teachings and study more texts, but still mix these activities with our own analysis and meditation. We should take care that the text we use are authentic ones written by those who are skilled in the subject, because anything good always has its shoddy imitations. We should not dismiss the views of the lower schools, but rather practise trying to see things from their perspectives. Sharpening our mind on subtle impermanence and selflessness as put forward in the lower schools' systems is an excellent preparation for cutting through the unequalled Consequentialist insights. In meditation we can start with the lowest school and try to work up to the view of the highest school. It is also very useful to perform this type of meditation in reverse order, starting off with the most subtle object of refutation and working down the scale to the grossest.

Whatever dharma practice we engage in, whether it is practising analytical meditation based on reasoning, or placement meditation, where one focuses the mind only on one object, whether one is practising moral discipline, or accumulating merit by helping others, what one should never do is eagerly expect some marvellous effect in just a short time. 'Abandon the hope of results' is excellent advice. Grasping at achieving dharma realizations is a sure way to prevent them occurring and can lead to all sorts of false pride or despondency. We should try to strive to do our best and attain the goals that Buddha talked about without having fixed ideas about when we hope to achieve anything. What we need is a stable and firm type of practice. What we have in our minds at the moment are very firm and stable tendencies towards various delusions. When we practise dharma we try to build up predispositions towards virtuous states of mind and towards wisdom. If we practise well over a long period of time then these latter kinds of predispositions will become stable and strong. If someone carved a Buddha image out of a boulder, then we would expect it to last for a long time. On the other hand if he or she simply painted a Buddha image on the rock, less effort would be involved but the rain and the other elements would soon get to work and destroy it. In our dharma practice we should aim to be like the person who sculptures the stone, making the extra effort required to bring forth a Buddha out of the rough rock by patient chiselling, for the sake of a more enduring result.

Even though the seeds of delusion sprout profusely in our minds at the moment, since these delusions are based on misunderstanding of reality, they cannot after all be impossible to get rid of. As soon as we achieve a clear understanding, our ignorance must give way like darkness before light. The predispositions we place on our mindstream when we meditate on dependent-arising are very stable because they are based on reality. So even if these predispositions do not ripen up into a realization of dependent-arising in this lifetime, because they are based on the truth and have some stability, there is every reason to hope they will ripen up in a future existence. Then, by prolonged acquaintance with and meditation on this precious realization of dependent-arising, our delusions can be uprooted once and for all. Confident then, that the results of practising these teachings of the Enlightened One, passed down through Nagarjuna, Chandrakirti and Tsong Khapa will be very beneficial, we should enter into the practice of them with a relaxed and happy attitude. When we become more deeply acquainted with them we may reach the conclusion that there is nothing whatever more beneficial than them for sentient beings, in which case we will approach them in a mood of gladness and rejoicing. Howsoever, a feeling of pleasure when practising the dharma is worth a great deal. There are various reasons why we might be inclined to take these teachings very seriously; because they are very profound and need plenty of careful thought; because they are the gateway to the highest wisdom; because they precipitate a fundamental change of heart in us towards the allurements of cyclic existence. Nonetheless a tight or tense mind will only be a hindrance, so we should keep a happy mind at the beginning, in the middle and at the end.

Notes

1. One of the sources for this paragraph on Tsong Khapa's biography is the introduction to *Tsong Khapa's Speech of Gold in the Essence of True Eloquence*, by Robert Thurman. Much greater detail will be found there.

2. The Sanskrit and Tibetan names of the followers of the various Buddhist schools are as follows:

English	Sanskrit	Tibetan
Particularist	Vaibhashika	bye brag smra ba
Sutra-follower	Sautrantika	mdo sde pa
Proponents of Mind Only	Chittamatra	sems tsam pa
Proponents of the Middle Way	Madhyamika	dbu ma pa
Autonomist	Svatantrika	rang rgyud pa
Consequentialist	Prasangika	thal 'gyur pa

3. The Buddhist world view acknowledges the primacy of mind. In this view mind cannot arise out of a conglomeration of insensible material particles, during the process of embryonic development for instance. An individual's mind has experienced many previous lives before inhabiting the present body and the process of rebirth will go on until liberation is achieved.

4. The five physical sense powers are not identified as the sense organs themselves but as a kind of clear form located within them. They give to their respective consciousness the ability to apprehend and to be generated in the aspect of their respective objects. The sixth sense power, which empowers mental as opposed to sense consciousness, is not physical, but is a previous moment of consciousness. For further details see *Meditation on Emptiness* by Jeffrey Hopkins.

5. We noted earlier that in an ordinary person's continuum every one of his cognitions is affected by ignorance. But the fact an ordinary person's valid awareness is not totally free of the effects of ignorance does not mean that

it cannot be correct with respect to the main features of its object. For instance, we can still see and recognize a friend when we are wearing dark glasses which prevent us from seeing colours properly.

6. Permanent phenomena are those phenomena which do not change and are not produced from causes. In this sense they are static, but not necessarily eternal. Existence itself is permanent. So are instance and generality, not any particular instance or generality but instance and generality themselves. True cessation (the third noble truth), which is the absence of all delusions in a realized being's mindstream, is another example, as is uncaused space, defined as the absence of obstruction and contact.

7. For further details on how to conduct a basic meditation on the absence of inherent existence of the I, see the early sections of *Meditation on Emptiness* by Jeffrey Hopkins.

8. The Three Jewels are the three objects a Buddhist goes to for refuge. They are the Buddha or Enlightened One, the Dharma, his teaching and the Sangha, the community of those who have made progress on the path to enlightenment.

Bibliography
Tibetan and Sanskrit Works

Āryadeva ('phags pa lha, second to third century C.E.)

—*The Four Hundred: Treatise of the Four Hundred Stanzas*
—catuḥśatakaśāstrakārikā
—bstan bcos bzhi brgya pa zhes bya ba'i tshig le'ur byas pa

Chandrakirti (zla ba grags pa, seventh century)

—*Supplement to the Middle Way/ Supplement to (Nagarjuna's) Treatise on Middle way.*
—madhyamakavatara
—dbu ma la 'jug pa
—English translation (Ch. I-V): Jeffrey Hopkins in *Compassion in Tibetan Buddhism*, Valois, NY: Gabriel Snow Lion, 1980.
—English translation (Ch. VI): Stepehen Batchelor in Geshe Rabten's *Echoes of Voidness*. London: Wisdom, 1982.

Dharmakirti (chos kyi grags pa, seventh century)

—*Commentary on Valid Cognition/ Commentary on (Dignaga's) Compendium on Valid Cognition.*
—Pramanavartikakarika
—Tshad ma rnam 'grel gyi tshig le'ur byas pa

Nagarjuna (klu sgrub, first to second century CE)

—*Treatise on the Middle Way/ Fundamental Treatise on the Middle Way, Called 'Wisdom'*
—Madhyamaksastra/Prajnanamamulamadhyamaka-karika
—Dbu ma's bstan bcos/dbu ma rtsa ba'i tshig le'ur byas pa shes rab ces bya ba
—English translation: David J. Kalupahana, *Nagarjuna: The Philosophy of the Middle Way*. Albany: State University Press of New York, 1986.

Tsong Khapa 1357-1419)

> —*The Essence of Eloquent Speech: Treatise Distinguishing the Interpretable and the Definitive*
> —Drang ba dang nges pa'i don rnam par phye ba'i bstan bcos legs bshad snying po.
> —English Translation: Robert Thurman, *Tsong Khapa's Speech of Gold in the Essence of True Eloquence'*. Princeton, Princeton University Press, 1984. Reprint, Delhi: Motilal Banarsidass, 1989.

OTHER WORKS

Hopkins, Jeffrey, *Meditation on Emptiness*. London: Wisdom, 1983.

Thurman, Robert, *Tsong Khapa's Speech of Gold in the 'Essence of True Eloquence'*. Princeton: Princeton University Press, 1984. Reprint, Delhi: Motilal Banarsidass, 1989.